S0-BYH-030

free and clear

The Truth from the Book of Exodus to Your Life Today

By David Guzik

The grass withers, the flower fades,
but the word of our God stands forever.
Isaiah 40:8

Free and Clear
Copyright ©2019 by David Guzik
ISBN 1-56599-033-1
Printed in the United States of America
or in the United Kingdom

Enduring Word

5662 Calle Real #184

Goleta, CA 93117

Electronic Mail: ewm@enduringword.com

Internet Home Page: www.enduringword.com

**Cover photograph by Craig Brewer © 2004
www.craigbrewer.com**

All rights reserved. No portion of this book may be reproduced in any form (except for quotations in reviews) without the written permission of the publisher.

Scripture references, unless noted, are from the New King James Version of the Bible, copyright © 1979, 1980, 1982, Thomas Nelson, Inc., Publisher.

A FEW WORDS FROM THE AUTHOR

The Book of Exodus is about God's people escaping bondage, whatever form the bondage takes. Through God's work with ancient Israel we see how God sets people free. But Israel needed more than a release from their chains - they also needed to address the scars left by 400 years of slavery in Egypt. On the journey from Egypt and to the Promised Land of Canaan, God began their transformation from a slave people to a free people. He worked to clear Israel from their bondage of thinking and acting like slaves.

God wants you to be free and clear - not only free from the bondage of sin, but also clear of the lingering effects of your past slavery. My prayer is that by spending time on these important truths through Exodus, God will make you more free and more clear.

David Guzik
July 2004
Siegen, Germany

ONE

Reading from Exodus: Chapter 1

THE PRE-ARRANGED PRINCE

And the child grew, and she brought him to Pharaoh's daughter, and he became her son. So she called his name Moses, saying, "Because I drew him out of the water." (Exodus 2:10)

The baby Moses first opened his eyes to an unfriendly world. He was born in a superpower of a nation, but he was of an alien, oppressed race, during a time when all Hebrew boy babies were sentenced to death. But Moses had parents who really trusted God.

Exodus 6:20 says Moses' parents were named Amram and Jochebed. Jewish legends say that Moses' birth was painless for his mother and when he was born his face was so beautiful that the room was filled with light equal to the sun and moon combined. They say he walked and spoke when he was a day old, and refused to nurse, eating solid food from day one. All these are fanciful legends. The truth about Moses is amazing enough.

When the parents of Moses defied the order of Pharaoh and saved their child, they were motivated by more than the natural affection of parents. According to Hebrews 11:23, they did it also out of faith in God. But in a literal sense, Moses' mother did *exactly* what Pharaoh said to do – he said to put the boy babies in the river. However, she took care to put him in a waterproofed basket and then she strategically floated him in the river. Most of all, Moses' parents are great examples of entrusting the child's welfare and future to God alone. When Moses' mother let go of the little boat she made of bulrushes, she gave up something precious, trusting that God would take care of her gift, and perhaps God would find a way to give it back to her.

God worked it all out. Pharaoh's daughter found baby Moses, and then she hired Moses' own mother to take care of the baby! Not only did Moses' mother get to care for her own child, she also got *paid* for it. So God greatly rewarded the faith of Moses' mother, both as she trusted Him as she hid Moses for three months, and then as she trusted Him by setting Moses out on the river.

Being the adopted son of Pharaoh's daughter, Moses was in the royal family. Josephus says he was the heir to the throne of Egypt, and that while a young man, Moses lead the armies of Egypt in victorious battle against the Ethiopians. Certainly, he was raised with both the science and learning of Egypt. Acts 7:22 says, "*Moses was learned in all the wisdom of the Egyptians, and was mighty in words and deeds.*" Egypt was one of the most academic and scientific societies on the earth at that time. In the best schools Moses learned geography, history, grammar and writing, literature, philosophy, and music.

When Moses went somewhere, he traveled in a princely chariot, and his guards cried out "bow the knee!" If he floated on the Nile, it was in an ancient yacht, with musical accompaniment – he lived the royal life. But Moses was certainly also raised in the Hebrew heritage of his mother. He was raised in a special environment with a special set of life circumstances, circumstances that God would use to work out His perfect will through Moses.

You aren't Moses, but God has also allowed the unique circumstances of your life for a purpose. Today, as you think about what God has allowed to come into your life, trust Him to work His loving purpose through it all.

TWO
Reading from Exodus: Chapter 2

THE RIGHT KIND OF PREPARATION

And he saw an Egyptian beating a Hebrew, one of his brethren. So he looked this way and that way, and when he saw no one, he killed the Egyptian and hid him in the sand. And when he went out the second day, behold, two Hebrew men were fighting, and he said to the one who did the wrong, 'Why are you striking your companion?' Then he said, "Who made you a prince and a judge over us? Do you intend to kill me as you killed the Egyptian?" So Moses feared and said, "Surely this thing is known!" (Exodus 2:11-14)

According to Acts 7:23, this happened when Moses was 40 years old. For all his 40 years before this, Moses was trained and groomed to become the next Pharaoh of Egypt, all the while being made aware of his true origins by his mother. On this occasion, Moses was certainly right in preventing the beating of one of his Hebrew brethren. Yet at the same time this was perhaps a premature attempt to fulfill his destiny - to *make himself* the deliverer of Israel from Egypt's bondage in the way that made sense to him. Acts 7:25 shows us exactly where Moses' heart was: *For he supposed that his brethren would have understood that God would deliver them by his hand, but they did not understand.*

If Moses ever sat down and decided to deliver his people from their Egyptian bondage, he would never think this way: "My brother Aaron and I will go to Pharaoh with a special stick that turns into a snake. We'll ask him to let us go back to Canaan, and if he says no, we'll bring plagues of blood in the

Nile River, frogs, mosquitoes, flies, cattle disease, boils, hail, locusts, and darkness. If all that doesn't work, we'll kill all the firstborn of Egypt and escape across the Red Sea, which will part for us and flow back to drown the Egyptians. Then we'll cross the wilderness and come to Canaan." Instead of that plan – which turned out to be God's plan – Moses planned the deliverance of Israel the way any man would, and logically saw himself as the deliverer, because of his accepted leadership among the Egyptians. The only problem was that God was going to accomplish this deliverance and use Moses in a way that no man would ever dream of!

Why did God allow all this? Moses had no idea of it at the time, but he was *too big* for God to use. Moses tried to do the Lord's work in man's wisdom and power. It wouldn't work. After 40 years of seemingly perfect preparation, Moses had another 40 years of seemingly meaningless waiting in order to perfect God's preparation.

In addition, Moses' leadership was not accepted by the Jewish people as a whole, even though God made him a prince and a judge over them. Moses, like Jesus, was rejected by Israel at his "first coming." Both Moses and Jesus were favored by God from birth, both were miraculously preserved in childhood, both were mighty in words and deed, both offered deliverance to Israel, both were rejected, and rejected with spite, both with Israel denying that they had any right to be ruler and a judge over them.

Just like Jesus, Moses could not be a deliverer when he lived in the palaces of glory. He had to come down off the throne, away from the palace, into a humble place before he could deliver his people. Remember today that our Savior left His exalted palace and place of privilege to save His people – and see how Moses is a "preview" of Jesus. Then ask: are you also willing to let God use you in your humility?

THREE
Reading from Exodus: Chapter 3

YOUR ATTENTION PLEASE

So when the LORD saw that he turned aside to look, God called to him from the midst of the bush and said, "Moses, Moses!" And he said, "Here I am." (Exodus 3:4)

The Bible tells us that at the time God got the attention of Moses, Moses kept the sheep belonging to his father-in-law. The grammar of the original Hebrew suggests that keeping sheep was his occupation for a long time. By now, it was 40 years that Moses lived as an obscure shepherd out in the desert. At this point, his life was so humble, he didn't even have a flock of sheep to call his own – the sheep belonged to his father-in-law Jethro.

One day Moses brought the sheep to Horeb, which was called "the mountain of God." This mountain is also later called Mount Sinai. The name *Horeb* means "desert" or "desolation," and this gives an idea of the kind of land Moses worked in. Out in the middle of this nowhere, Moses saw something amazing: a bush burning, but not burnt up. It caught fire but it wasn't consumed.

It wasn't just that Moses saw a bush on fire. Apparently, it is not uncommon for plants like this to spontaneously ignite in the desert. But two things were distinctive about this bush. First, the *Angel of the LORD* appeared from the midst of the bush. Second, though the bush burned it was not consumed. The bush burning but not burnt up was a magnetic sight to Moses. It drew him in for a closer examination. Some say that this burning bush was a picture of God's grace, which draws us to Him.

Look at the picture. This was a thorn-bush, because the original Hebrew word describing it comes from the word "to stick" or "to prick," so it means a thorn-bush or a bramble bush. Thorns are a figure of the curse, because Adam was cursed to bring forth thorns and thistles from the earth, according to Genesis 3:18. So we have a picture of the curse being burned (a picture of judgment) yet without being consumed (a picture of God's mercy and grace).

But the miraculous sight in itself didn't accomplish God's purpose. God didn't speak to Moses until He had Moses' attention. It says it was **when the LORD saw that he turned** that God spoke to Moses. There can be amazing, miraculous things going on all around us. But God often won't speak to us until we turn to Him and listen. What has God allowed in your life to turn you towards Him?

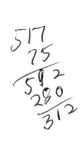

FOUR
Reading from Exodus: Chapter 3

COME INTO MY HOUSE

Then He said, "Do not draw near this place. Take your sandals off your feet, for the place where you stand is holy ground." (Exodus 3:5)

Moses was raised in a royal family and groomed for national leadership. At the same time, he had a sense of God's call and destiny for his life. After a futile attempt to fulfill that destiny in his own strength and wisdom, Moses ran for his life. He ended up tending someone else's sheep on the backside of some of the most desolate wilderness you'll find anywhere. After 40 years, God got Moses' attention with a bush that burned yet was not consumed. Once God had his attention, He told Moses to do two things.

First, God told Moses to keep a distance (**Do not draw near this place**). In the original language, the phrase **do not draw near** literally has the sense of "stop coming closer." Moses was on his way for an up-close examination of this burning bush when God stopped him short. Why did God tell him, "stop coming closer"? Because this was a holy place. Because God is a holy God, there will always be a distance between God and man. Even if a man were a perfect man, he would never be equal to God. God isn't just a "super-man." God is God.

Second, God told Moses to show a reverence for God's presence (**Take your sandals off your feet**). The ground was holy because God's immediate presence was there. But why did God tell Moses to take off his sandals? First, removing the sandals showed an appropriate humility. In the days of Moses the poorest and most needy had no shoes and servants usually went barefoot. It was a way for Moses to humble himself before the LORD.

Second, taking the sandals off also recognized the immediate presence of God. If you travel and visit other cultures you know that in many places, it is good manners to take off your shoes when you come into someone's house. Because the LORD demonstrated His unique presence at the burning bush, now Moses was in God's "house." Taking off the shoes was both an expression of humility and *an invitation for fellowship.*

The two are always connected. When we humble ourselves before God, we can and will draw closer to Him. *God resists the proud, but gives grace to the humble* (James 4:6). There is a sure-fire way to draw closer to God: recognize Him as bigger in your eyes and make yourself smaller. Take your shoes off when you come into His presence.

FIVE
Reading from Exodus: Chapter 3

DO YOU REMEMBER?

Moreover He said, "I am the God of your father; the God of Abraham, the God of Isaac, and the God of Jacob." And Moses hid his face, for he was afraid to look upon God. (Exodus 3:6)

For the first 40 years of his life Moses was raised in a royal family and groomed for national leadership. For the second 40 years of his life he tended someone else's sheep out in a desolate wilderness. In between was a futile attempt to fulfill God's destiny for his life his own way, instead of letting God do it His way.

Now God had the attention of this 80-year-old man, standing in front of a bush that was on fire but not burnt up. God spoke to Moses out of this burning bush, and after calling his name and telling him to take off his sandals, the LORD told Moses exactly who He was.

Who was this God who spoke to Moses out of the burning bush? He described Himself as, **the God of your father; the God of Abraham, the God of Isaac, and the God of Jacob**. Abraham, Isaac, and Jacob were the ancestors of the Jewish people, known as the "patriarchs." They lived some 400 years before Moses and their stories are told in the book of Genesis. In Genesis, we read that God made many promises to Abraham, Isaac, and Jacob and to their descendants. God promised them a *land* (the Promised Land of Israel), a *nation*, and a *blessing* that would come through them to the whole world.

God could have identified Himself to Moses in almost any way. But He chose to say, **I am the God of your father; the God of Abraham, the God of Isaac, and the God of Jacob** because He wanted Moses to know that He remembered these 400 year-old promises. Moses, like all the Jewish people at that time, probably felt that God had neglected His covenant for those 400 years. But even in that time, God was at work preserving and multiplying the nation.

God had a special relationship with Abraham, Isaac, and Jacob. But the Lord will reveal Himself to Moses more intimately than He did to any of the patriarchs. Yet it all began when God reminded Moses of the promises made to the patriarchs. Those promises were like a bridge that Moses and God met upon.

Moses responded by hiding his face in fear, as a man who knew he was not only a creature, but a sinful creature. In his 40 years tending sheep, Moses must have spent many lonely days and nights troubled in his conscience about his murder of an Egyptian, of his pride in thinking that he could deliver Israel himself, of a thousand other sins, both real and imagined. But God was ready to forgive and He wanted Moses to put all that away and get on with knowing and serving Him.

Moses' humbleness before God was a good thing. But his crippled, guilty conscience was a bad thing. Hebrews 9:14 makes this challenge: *How much more shall the blood of Christ, who through the eternal Spirit offered Himself without spot to God, cleanse your conscience from dead works to serve the living God?* We, like Moses, need to be reminded that God is the God of the covenant, and His covenant is a promise to forgive and restore. Afraid as he was, God wasn't done with Moses yet, and God isn't done with you.

SIX

Reading from Exodus: Chapter 3

ANSWER ENOUGH

But Moses said to God, "Who am I that I should go to Pharaoh, and that I should bring the children of Israel out of Egypt?" So He said, "I will certainly be with you."
(Exodus 3:11-12)

For his first 40 years, Moses believed his destiny was to be the deliverer of Israel. All that vanished when he fled as a fugitive from his position of privilege, escaping to the desolate wilderness. Then God appeared to Moses, speaking from a bush that flamed but did not burn. The LORD invited Moses to fulfill his dreamed-of destiny, and now Moses wasn't so certain. After 40 years in the wilderness he asked, **Who am I that I should go to Pharaoh?**

Forty years before this Moses thought he knew who he was. He was a prince of Egypt and a Hebrew, God's chosen instrument for the deliverance of Israel. But after 40 years of chasing sheep around the desert, Moses didn't have the same self-sure confidence that he once had. Could God still use him? Of course God could, but first the Lord had to set Moses' focus where it had to be.

God replied by taking Moses' focus off of where it was (himself) and on to where it should be (God). God never responded to Moses' question **Who am I?** Instead, He reminded Moses, **I will certainly be with you.** This was a great opportunity to deal with Moses' self-esteem problem. We notice that God ignored the solutions we usually run to regarding the problem of self-esteem. But Moses did not have a self-esteem problem when he asked **Who am I?** He only had a self-esteem problem when he was too confident in his *own* ability to deliver Israel.

Who am I? wasn't the right question. The right question was "Who is God?" The truth about God was far more important than the truth about Moses. When we know the God who is with us, we can step forth confidently to do His will. Daniel 11:32 says, *the people who know their God shall be strong, and carry out great exploits.* Knowing Moses better wasn't the key for Moses. Knowing God better was the key. It's also the key for each one of us.

In Ephesians 4:20-21, Paul challenged Christians to a God-honoring lifestyle by reminding them of their knowledge of Jesus. He wrote: *But you have not so learned Christ, if indeed you have heard Him and have been taught by Him.* This shows that the Ephesians *learned Christ*, not only learning *about* Jesus, but also learning *Him.* This means a living, abiding knowledge of Jesus will keep us faithful to Him and keep us willing to take the kind of big steps of faith God called Moses to take. It's all rooted in knowing God, and knowing Him as He is revealed in Jesus.

Charles Spurgeon said it well: "So, if you want to know the Lord Jesus Christ, you must live with him. First he must himself speak to you, and afterwards you must abide in him. He must be the choice companion of your morning hours, he must be with you throughout the day, and with him you must also close the night; and as often as you may wake during the night, you must say, 'When I awake, I am still with thee.'"

SEVEN
Reading from Exodus: Chapters 3-4

TELL THEM WHO SENT YOU

*Thus you shall say to the children of Israel,
"I Am has sent me to you."* (Exodus 3:14)

God gave Moses a big job to do. He told Moses to lead the people of Israel out of Egypt to Mount Sinai and then to the Promised Land. Before Moses could confront Pharaoh, he had to first gain the confidence of his fellow Israelites. The first thing they would ask is, "Who sent you, anyway?" God told Moses just how to respond.

Forty years before, Moses probably would answer that question by looking at himself. He might have said, "What do you mean, 'Who sent me?' I'm Moses, from the house of Pharaoh! I'm a prince of Egypt!" But forty years of tending sheep took away his sense of self-reliance. He would have to trust God's answer to the question.

God told Moses His name was I AM - because God simply is. There was never a time when God did not exist or a time when He will cease to exist. The name I AM has within it the idea that God is completely independent; that He relies on nothing or no one (as in Isaiah 40:28-29 or John 5:26). God doesn't need anybody or anything for life or existence - He *is* life.

Another idea in the name I AM is the sense that God is "the becoming one." God becomes whatever is lacking in our time of need. The name I AM invites us to fill in the blank to meet our need. When we are in darkness, Jesus says "I AM the light." When we are hungry, He says "I AM the bread of life." When we are defenseless, He says "I AM the Good Shepherd." God is the becoming one, becoming what we need at the moment.

Those were Moses' credentials. He represented this great God, the I AM of Israel. The credentials of Moses did not bring honor to himself, but to the Lord. Moses had to give up his personal ambition of greatness and be content to be a representative of the great God.

God had a great work in front of Moses, and there were not enough resources in Moses to do the job. The power, wisdom, and endurance was not in Moses, it was all in the God who sent him. To have the I AM behind you is enough. God is for you. The I AM is behind you, and ready to be what you need Him to be. He is still the Becoming One.

EIGHT
Reading from Exodus: Chapter 4

USING WHAT IS AT HAND

So the LORD said to him, "What is that in your hand?"
(Exodus 4:2)

Moses had a big job to do, and he certainly couldn't do it alone. He could never bring the children of Israel out of Egypt without the support of the leaders of Israel. But when he came back to the people of Israel after being gone for 40 years, how would they ever have confidence in him? God gave Moses three signs to demonstrate his divine credentials to the leaders of Israel. But the demonstration began with a simple question: **What is that in your hand?**

The question reflects a precious principle of the way God uses people; *God used what Moses had in his hand.* Moses' years of tending sheep were not useless, because those years put into his hand the things he could use for God's glory.

This is the way God often works.

• God used the sharp stick in Shamgar's hand (Judges 3:31).

• God used the sling in David's hand (1 Samuel 17:49).

• God used the jawbone of a donkey in Samson's hand (Judges 15:15).

• God used five loaves and two fish in the hands of a little boy (John 6:9).

Forty years before this Moses held a royal scepter in his hand. God didn't use the royal scepter but He did use the simple shepherd's staff. Later, that rod of Moses would split the Red Sea. It would strike a rock and see water pour forth.

It would be raised over battle until Israel was victorious. God thought a lot of that stick that Moses carried in his hand. That simple staff that Moses held on to for so many years would come to be called "the rod of God" (Exodus 4:20; 17:9).

What has God put in your hand? It might be a gift or a talent or a resource that you don't think very much of. Moses didn't walk around admiring the rod he carried in his hand. But God used it for great glory. You may think God has to put something new or different in your hand before He can use you. But right now, God has put *something* in your hand that He can use. You have some gift, some interest, some ability that marks your life. God wants to ask you the same question He asked Moses: **What is that in your hand?** The answer may reveal how God wants to use you today.

NINE

THREE SIGNS AND YOU'RE OUT

Then it will be, if they do not believe you, nor heed the message of the first sign, that they may believe the message of the latter sign. And it shall be, if they do not believe even these two signs, or listen to your voice, that you shall take water from the river and pour it on the dry land. And the water which you take from the river will become blood on the dry land.
(Exodus 4:8-9)

Moses was on a mission from God, but it was a mission that involved many more people than just Moses. Therefore he had to persuade the rest of the people of Israel that he really was on a mission from God. Moses couldn't lead them out of Egypt unless they wanted to go. He had to prove himself to them, and God gave Moses three signs to make the proof.

The first sign was for Moses to take his shepherd's staff, throw it on the ground, and God would miraculously change the staff into a real snake. Then Moses was to pick up the snake by the tail (always a dangerous thing to do) and the snake would turn into a shepherd's staff again.

The second sign was for Moses to take his hand and put it inside his robe. When he pulled it out, it would be white with leprosy. When he put the leprous hand back in his robe and pulled it out again, God promised that it would be just as healthy as before.

Each of the first two signs had to do with conversion. In each, something good and useful (a rod or a hand) was converted to something evil (a serpent or a leprous hand).

Then, by a miracle, it was converted back into something good and useful again.

There was a real message in the first two signs. The first sign said, "Moses, if you obey Me, your enemies will be made powerless." The second sign said, "Moses, if you obey Me, your pollution can be made pure." God gave Moses these signs because he was worried in both areas. He thought, "I can't go back to Egypt because I have enemies there." He thought, "I can't go back to Egypt because I have a criminal record there." Before these signs touched the heart of anyone else, they touched Moses' heart. This is always the pattern with God's leaders. They can't touch the hearts of others unless their hearts are touched first.

The third sign was simply a sign of judgment. Good, pure waters were made foul and bloody by the work of God - and they did not become pure again. If the miracles of conversion did not turn the hearts of the people, then perhaps the sign of judgment would. But the sign of judgment was only given when unbelief persisted in the face of the previous miracles of conversion.

God has put miracles of conversion right in front of your eyes. Perhaps He has even put a miracle of conversion in the mirror! Learn from God's miracles of conversion, and trust Him. Then He won't have to teach you through a sign of judgment.

ABLE OR WILLING?

"Now therefore, go, and I will be with your mouth and teach you what you shall say." But he said, "O my Lord, please send by the hand of whomever else You may send." So the anger of the LORD was kindled against Moses.
(Exodus 4:12-14)

God had a job for Moses to do. Forty years earlier Moses would have jumped at the chance, but now he was hesitant. To answer his hesitation, God gave Moses assurance after assurance. He gave Moses the sign of the burning bush. He allowed Moses to hear the divine voice. He gave Moses the divine name. He gave Moses three miraculous signs. It still wasn't enough to assure Moses. Finally, God gave Moses a *command*: **Now therefore, go, and I will be with your mouth and teach you what you shall say**.

Moses finally finished with all the excuses and he declared the fact of his heart: he would much rather that God send someone else. Despite all his excuses, Moses' problem wasn't really a lack of ability; it was a lack of willingness.

God reacted to Moses and his excuse: **So the anger of the LORD was kindled against Moses**.

God was not angry when Moses asked, *Who am I?* (Exodus 3:11).

God was not angry when Moses asked, *Who should I say sent me?* (Exodus 3:13).

God was not angry when Moses disbelieved God's Word and said *suppose they will not believe me or listen to my voice?* (Exodus 4:1).

God was not angry even when Moses (falsely) claimed that he was not and had never been eloquent (Exodus 4:10).

But God was angry when Moses was just plain unwilling.

There may be a hundred reasons why Moses was unwilling. Some of those reasons probably made a lot of sense. But the bottom line was that Moses was *unwilling*, not *unable*.

More than anything, God wants us to be willing. Willing to do what He tells us to do. Willing to serve Him. Willing to listen.

God regards your willingness as a serious matter. Do you?

ELEVEN
Reading from Exodus: Chapter 4

BUT DID YOU GO?

So Moses went. (Exodus 4:18)

Three simple words, but there is a lot of power behind them: **So Moses went**.

Moses had a dramatic experience with God out in the desert. God met him in a miracle – a bush aflame, yet not being burnt up. The voice of God speaking directly to Moses. Three miraculous signs.

But when the fire fades from the burning bush, when the voice of God is silent across the desert; then it is upon us to obey, and to do what God told us to do. More than one person has a spectacular "burning bush" experience and then carries on as if it had never happened.

Moses was different. **So Moses went**. God has poured a lot into you, and given you a call and a promise. But did you go? God has put people on your heart and needs before your eyes. But did you go? He has told you to stay awhile and wait. But did you go?

Sometimes we won't do what God tells us because we don't see how it will all work out. But Moses didn't have any idea what he was getting into when he agreed to take the LORD's call.

He couldn't see the Egyptian army closing in, and God parting the Red Sea through Moses' hand.

He couldn't see the song of victory, the water from the rock, the manna from heaven, the battles won through prayer.

He couldn't see a vision of God on Mount Sinai, the voice of God from heaven, the tablets of stone, the golden calf.

He couldn't see the tabernacle built, the priests consecrated.

He couldn't see the spies sent into Canaan, the response of unbelief, and a thirty-eight year sentence to wander the wilderness.

Moses couldn't see a lonely climb to the top of Mount Pisgah, where he would die looking out over the land of promise.

He couldn't see the honor of sitting beside the Lord on the Mount of Transfiguration.

Did Moses have any idea what he was getting into? Not really. But, **Moses went**. In the same way, we should not demand to know the path ahead before we go. Hearing God's instruction is enough.

TWELVE
Reading from Exodus: Chapter 4

HARD HEARTS MADE SOFT

And the LORD said to Moses, "When you go back to Egypt, see that you do all those wonders before Pharaoh which I have put in your hand. But I will harden his heart, so that he will not let the people go." (Exodus 4:21)

Moses was almost on his way. But before he left the wilderness to return to Egypt, God wanted him to know something important. He would show these signs to Pharaoh, and make these requests to him, but Pharaoh would not listen. In fact, the LORD said, **I will harden his heart, so that he will not let the people go**.

What happened here? Is it fair for God to harden a man's heart?

Look at the whole picture. Sometimes it says that God hardened the heart of Pharaoh (Exodus 4:21). Sometimes it says that Pharaoh hardened his own heart (Exodus 8:15). Sometimes it says simply that Pharaoh's heart was hardened, without saying who did it (Exodus 7:13).

So which description is true? How did it really happen? All three are true. But when we consider the occasions where God hardened Pharaoh's heart, we must never think that God did it *against* Pharaoh's will. It was never a case of Pharaoh saying, "Oh, I want to do what is good and right and I want to bless these people of Israel" and God replying, "Not so Pharaoh, for I will harden your heart against them!"

When God hardened Pharaoh's heart, He allowed Pharaoh's heart to do what Pharaoh wanted to do - God gave Pharaoh over to his sin (after the pattern of Romans 1:18-32).

All God has to do to harden hearts is give the sinful heart what it wants. What we need is a *new* heart. In Ezekiel 36:26, God made a precious promise: *I will give you a new heart and put a new spirit within you; I will take the heart of stone out of your flesh and give you a heart of flesh.*

What is the condition of your heart before God? If you are tired of your hard heart, you can ask God to change it. And don't think you can blame Him for your hard heart, because He just gave you what you wanted. No one has ever come to God looking for a soft heart and instead received a hard heart.

God showed His mercy to Moses by telling him what he was up against from the beginning. Moses wouldn't be surprised that Pharaoh rejected him. Let the LORD show you that He is in control, and give Him control of your heart today.

THIRTEEN
Reading from Exodus: Chapter 5

WHERE THE REAL POWER IS

*Afterward Moses and Aaron went in and told Pharaoh,
"Thus says the L*ORD *God of Israel: 'Let My people go, that they
may hold a feast to Me in the wilderness.'"* (Exodus 5:1)

Moses wasn't asking for a little favor. This was a big one.
To appreciate how audacious Moses' request was, we must
understand the power and authority the Egyptian Pharaohs
claimed to have. They said every Pharaoh was the child of
the sun and that he was a friend to the greatest gods of Egypt
and sat with them in their own temples to receive worship
alongside them. A Pharaoh was anything but a public servant;
the entire public lived to serve the Pharaoh. His power and
authority were supreme, and there was no constitution or law
or legislature higher or even remotely equal to him.

An inscription by a Pharaoh on an ancient Egyptian
temple gives us the idea. It reads, "I am that which was, and
is, and shall be, and no man has lifted my veil." The Pharaoh
was believed to be more than a man. He thought he was a
god, and the Egyptians agreed. This was what Moses was up
against.

After Moses had the remarkable encounter at the burning
bush and after he saw God turn the hearts of the leaders
of Israel towards him, Moses now had to confront the real
enemy: Pharaoh.

Moses must have felt strange walking into Pharaoh's palace
on the day he came to speak to the ruler of Egypt. He once
walked those same palaces as a prince, and might have one

day sat on the same throne the present Pharaoh did – yet, *esteeming the reproach of Christ greater riches than the treasures in Egypt; for he looked to the reward* (Hebrews 11:26). Moses knew both man's power and God's power, and he knew that in God he was more powerful than Pharaoh was.

As far as the human eye could see, it was Pharaoh against Moses. If the ancient world took bets and placed odds on a contest like that, Pharaoh would have been the odds-on favorite. It looked like he held all the power and all the advantage. But it's never smart to bet against God. He wins no matter what the odds. You can be confident in His power today.

FOURTEEN
Reading from Exodus: Chapter 5

WORSE BEFORE BETTER

So the same day Pharaoh commanded the taskmasters of the people and their officers, saying, "You shall no longer give the people straw to make brick as before. Let them go and gather straw for themselves. And you shall lay on them the quota of bricks which they made before. You shall not reduce it. For they are idle; therefore they cry out, saying, 'Let us go and sacrifice to our God.' Let more work be laid on the men, that they may labor in it, and let them not regard false words."
(Exodus 5:6-9)

The people of Israel were slaves in Egypt for 400 years. After 400 years, you may not like your slavery, but you are familiar with it. After that long, most people adjust to their slave conditions. Now at God's appointed time came a man named Moses. He used to be a prince in Egypt; perhaps even heir to the throne. But that was 40 years ago, when Moses fled Egypt on the heels of a murder rap. Now he came back and brought this message to the millions of Israelite slaves in Egypt: "God sent me to be your deliverer. I'm going to free you from this slavery and take you out of Egypt, and to your own country where you will never be slaves again."

If you were the common Israelite in Egpyt, hearing this would make you feel excited. It sounds great to be free from slavery. But when the common Israelite went to work the next day, things were *worse*, not better. Moses made his dramatic request to Pharaoh: "Let my people go!" At first Moses only asked for three days off so they could go and worship God in the wilderness. But Pharaoh not only rejected the idea of giving the Israelites three days off; he saw the request itself as a waste of good working time.

So, Pharaoh punished Israel because Moses made the request. He must have said, "Well Moses, you Israelites seem to have enough time to make these crazy requests – then you must have enough time to do more work." So Pharaoh commanded that the Israelites must gather their own materials (specifically, straw) for making bricks. In that day straw was an important ingredient in bricks because the acidic content of the straw made the bricks stronger.

After Moses' first works as the deliverer of Israel the children of Israel were in a worse place than before. After the first interview with Pharaoh Moses' leadership didn't make anything better at all. This was very disappointing to a people who had their hopes raised for deliverance from slavery.

Don't be surprised when you get right with God and look to His Deliverer (Jesus), and then things seem to get *worse* right away. God has just begun to work, and the big danger is giving up because of discouragement. Don't let it happen. God wanted to do something greater than transport a people from Egypt to Canaan; He wanted to take a people with the hearts and minds of slaves and give them the hearts and minds of His holy, chosen people. If it has to get a little worse before it gets better to accomplish that great purpose, then so be it.

FIFTEEN
Reading from Exodus: Chapter 5

DON'T ROCK THE BOAT?

Then, as they came out from Pharaoh, they met Moses and Aaron who stood there to meet them. And they said to them, "Let the LORD look on you and judge, because you have made us abhorrent in the sight of Pharaoh and in the sight of his servants, to put a sword in their hand to kill us."
(Exodus 5:20-21)

Moses confronted Pharaoh and demanded that he let the people of Israel go. Pharaoh was less than enthusiastic at the demand. Instead of granting Moses' request, Pharaoh made it worse for the Israelite laborers. To this point, Moses' work for Israel made it harder for the Israelites, not better for them. Pharaoh was angry. The people of Israel were angry and more tired than ever. Moses was just plain discouraged.

Do you hear the complaint of the people? They said to Moses, **Let the LORD look on you and judge, because you have made us abhorrent in the sight of Pharaoh**. What was the crime of Moses and Aaron? They were accused of making the children of Israel **abhorrent in the sight of Pharaoh**. When Israel was an obedient slave to Pharaoh it was easy to think that somehow, the Pharaoh was their friend. Now that the idea of freedom entered the minds of the Israelites, Pharaoh showed how he felt about them all along. He hated them. If they agreed to be submissive slaves they could get along fine with Pharaoh. If they wanted to be free, he hated them.

Isn't this the same as our spiritual warfare with the enemy of our soul? Satan seems "friendly" to us when we accept his "lordship." Go with the flow and surrender to Satan and everything seems "peaceful" with him. But when we start to be free in Jesus he often will try to make life difficult for us. Each Christian simply has to accept this fact and value the freedom we can have in Jesus and reject the "peaceful bondage" that Satan offers.

When Moses first came to the people of Israel and offered them freedom they were excited. Exodus 4:31 says: *So the people believed; and when they heard that the LORD had visited the children of Israel and that He had looked on their affliction, then they bowed their heads and worshipped.* Earlier, when Moses first came to the people of Israel and spelled out the vision of freedom and the Promised Land, the Israelites were excited. Now the faith, excitement, and worship of chapter four left pretty quickly.

It's the same for many Christians, who can have joy when things are easy, but true maturity is evident when we have God's peace in the middle of battle. Despite whatever you might be facing, you can have joy and you can thank God for who He is, even if you don't understand what He is doing. You can have the peace of God even if the devil is rocking your boat.

SIXTEEN
Reading from Exodus: Chapters 5-6

NOT DONE BREAKING

*So Moses returned to the L*ORD *and said, "Lord, why have You brought trouble on this people? Why is it You have sent me? For since I came to Pharaoh to speak in Your name, he has done evil to this people; neither have You delivered Your people at all."* (Exodus 5:22-23)

Things weren't going well for Moses. After God dramatically called him to deliver the people of Israel Moses confronted Pharaoh and hoped God would open the door for Israel to leave. But Pharaoh slammed the door shut. When Moses said "Let my people go," Pharaoh said "I'll make them even more miserable." All this made the people of Israel angry and it confused and discouraged Moses. So Moses poured out His heart to God. **Lord, why have You brought trouble on this people? Why is it You have sent me?** For Moses, God wasn't making sense and nothing was going according to plan.

When you are confused and discouraged, it is good to pour out your feelings to God; but it is bad to forget God's promise. Back at the burning bush, God said: *But I am sure that the king of Egypt will not let you go, no, not even by a mighty hand. So I will stretch out My hand and strike Egypt with all My wonders which I will do in its midst; and after that he will let you go* (Exodus 3:19-20). As far as God was concerned everything was moving according to plan.

Even though God warned Moses about this ahead of time, it seems that Moses hoped it would all come easy. He hoped that he would ask, Pharaoh would say yes, and God would be glorified. But it didn't work the way Moses thought it should. In this tough time the same old fears come crashing in on Moses: "I'm not the man God should send." "God won't come through." "Pharaoh and the Egyptians are too strong." There was still unbelief and lack of focus on God that had to be cleared out of Moses.

F.B. Meyer wrote of this time in Moses' life:

"The agony of soul through which Moses passed must have been as death to him. He died to his self-esteem, to his castle-building, to pride in his miracles, to the enthusiasm of his people, to everything that a popular leader loves. As he lay there on the ground alone before God, wishing himself back in Midian, and thinking himself hardly used, he was falling as a grain of wheat into the ground to die, no longer to abide alone, but to bear much fruit."

Moses probably thought that all the dying to himself was finished after 40 years of tending sheep in the desert of Midian; but the death to self wasn't over. It never is. God still will use adversity to train us to trust in Him until the day we go to be with Him in heaven. If that's discouraging to you, then come back to a trust in a loving God who knows you better than you know yourself.

SEVENTEEN
Reading from Exodus: Chapters 7-9

A PLAGUE ON YOUR HOUSE

Thus says the LORD: "By this you shall know that I am the LORD. Behold, I will strike the waters which are in the river with the rod that is in my hand, and they shall be turned to blood." (Exodus 7:17)

This describes the first of ten plagues that came against Pharaoh and Egypt until Pharaoh was willing to let Israel go without condition. Why did God plan it this way? What was the LORD trying to prove? The plagues accomplished many things:

The plagues answered Pharaoh's question, *"Who is the LORD?"* (Exodus 5:2), by showing that the LORD was greater than any of the false gods of Egypt.

The plagues displayed the power of God working through Moses, vindicating His representative (Exodus 9:16).

The plagues gave a testimony to the children of Israel for future generations (Exodus 10:2).

The plagues were a judgment against the false gods (really demons) of Egypt (Exodus 12:12, Numbers 33:4).

The plagues were a warning to the nations. More than 400 years later, the Philistines remembered the Lord God of Israel as the one who had plagued the Egyptians (1 Samuel 4:8).

The plagues were a testimony of the greatness of God to Israel (Exodus 15:11, Deuteronomy 4:34).

For all these reasons God sent blood in the waters of the Nile, frogs, lice, flies, disease on livestock, hail, locusts, and a supernatural darkness upon Egypt until He accomplished His purpose. The LORD God made it clear that He was greater than any of the Egyptian gods:

- Greater than Khnum (the guardian of the Nile).
- Greater than Hapi (the spirit of the Nile).
- Greater than Osiris (the giver of life who had the Nile as his bloodstream).
- Greater than Heqt (the frog-goddess of fertility).
- Greater than Hathor (a cow-like mother goddess).
- Greater than Imhotep (the god of medicine).
- Greater than Nut (the sky goddess).
- Greater than the gods as a whole, in that He could stop the whole worship of the Egyptian gods with loathsome lice and swarms of insects.
- Greater than Seth (thought to be the protector of crops).

God did for Pharaoh what He wants to do in our life: expose and topple every false god. When we trust in these gods, it is painful to have them put down; but it is always best to have them exposed. Today, ask God to show you the things in your life that are even close to being false gods, and put them away now. Don't push the LORD to plague your house.

EIGHTEEN
Reading from Exodus: Chapters 10-12

WHEN I SEE THE BLOOD

Now the blood shall be a sign for you on the houses where you are. And when I see the blood, I will pass over you; and the plague shall not be on you to destroy you when I strike the land of Egypt. (Exodus 12:13)

Pharaoh resisted God's call to let the people of Israel go. The LORD sent plague after plague to get the message across but Pharaoh didn't listen. So God declared one final plague: the Angel of the LORD would go throughout the land of Egypt and kill the firstborn of every family – every family that was not protected by the sacrificial blood of a lamb.

For Israel to be spared the judgment on the firstborn, they had to apply the blood just as God said they should. The blood of the lamb was essential to what God required. If an Israelite home didn't do what God told them to do with the blood of a lamb they were not protected. They could sacrifice the lamb and eat it; but without applying the blood, the family would still be visited by God's judgment. By the same token, if an Egyptian home believed in the power of the blood of the lamb and they made a proper Passover sacrifice, they were spared the judgment. The only thing that held back God's hand of judgment was the blood of the lamb.

When the ministry of Jesus first began, John the Baptist looked at Jesus and said *Behold, the Lamb of God who takes away the sins of the world* (John 1:29). Jesus is our Passover Lamb. He was without blemish. His death – represented by His blood – was done on our behalf. We have to do more than *know* that Jesus died for us. We have to do more than embrace Jesus in a superficial way. We have to do what He said to do with His blood – trust that it pays the penalty for our sin.

For the Israelites in the days of Moses, it was a bloody mess to take the blood of a lamb and dab it to the sides and top of your doorway. For Jesus, it was a bloody mess to die on a cross. But God can do something great even through a bloody mess. It isn't that God likes the gore, but He does insist that our sin be paid for. Since the God we sin against is a great God, the price to be paid is a great price. It's not that God likes to look at blood – but He does like to look at a price that has been paid, and the restoration with man that comes from a paid price.

At the end of it all there are only two ways people try to be right with God. Some try to be right based on what they can do for God, and some are right based on what God did for them in Jesus. Are you trusting in what you can do for God, or in what Jesus did for you? The blood is evidence of what He did for us.

NINETEEN
Reading from Exodus: Chapter 12

THE TWO PARTS OF REDEMPTION

You shall say, "It is the Passover sacrifice of the LORD, who passed over the houses of the children of Israel in Egypt when He struck the Egyptians and delivered our households." So the people bowed their heads and worshipped. (Exodus 12:27)

God's central act of redemption in the New Testament (and the whole Bible, for that matter) is what Jesus did for us on the cross. But before that the central act of redemption in the Old Testament was the deliverance of Israel from Egypt, at the time of the first Passover. Over and over again through the Old Testament God called Israel to remember Him as the God that brought them out of Egypt.

On that first Passover when Israel was delivered, their deliverance came in two ways. First, *an enemy was defeated.* Exodus 12:27 says, **He struck the Egyptians**. When God redeems us, He strikes out at the one who held us in cruel bondage. God struck the Egyptians, and the LORD struck Satan at the cross. Colossians 2:15 says of Jesus' work on the cross that He *disarmed principalities and powers, He made a public spectacle of them, triumphing over them in it.* Those "principalities and powers" are the devil and his demonic workers. When God redeems, He defeats the enemy that held us in bondage.

Second, *God rescues His people.* Exodus 12:27 says that the LORD **delivered our households**. It wouldn't matter much if the LORD struck their enemies but not deliver His people. But He does both. When the people of Israel came out of Egypt they had a new identity – they were no longer the slaves of Egypt; they were now the people of God.

God also gave them new promises. The old promise was, "I will give you the strength to endure this slavery." That is a great promise, but this is an even better one: "I will free you and give you your own Promised Land."

God also gave them a new walk. While they were slaves, the walked like slaves – head down, full of fear, with no confidence. Now, they could walk like free men and women, confident in God. God gave Israel a new life. He delivered them.

God does the same work of redemption today. When God redeems He strikes the enemy and rescues His people. In His deliverance, He gives us a new identity, new promises, and a new walk. Now it is simply up to us to live out what He gave to us.

TWENTY
Reading from Exodus: Chapters 12-13

NOW YOU KNOW

And it came to pass at midnight that the LORD struck all the firstborn in the land of Egypt, from the firstborn of Pharaoh who sat on his throne to the firstborn of the captive who was in the dungeon, and all the firstborn of livestock. (Exodus 12:29)

God knew it would come to this. At the beginning the LORD told Moses that Pharaoh would not let them go until he was forced to by the mighty works of God (Exodus 3:19-20). God told Moses that His work would somehow touch the firstborn of Egypt (Exodus 4:21-23). Now, the situation was about to end just as God said it would.

This final plague was directed against two of the most significant gods of Egypt. First it was against Osiris, the Egyptian god thought to be the giver of life. Secondly it was against the supposed deity of Pharaoh himself, because his own household was touched. We know from history that the house of Pharaoh was indeed stricken. An inscription was found in a shrine connected with the great Sphinx that records a solemn promise from the Egyptian gods that Thutmose IV would succeed his father, Amenhotep II, who was the pharaoh of the Exodus. It was considered normal for a Pharaoh's son to succeed his father, so it seemed strange that there would be such a special promise confirming this natural occurance.Undoubtedly, a public statement was needed because Thutmose IV was not his father's firstborn son - that son was struck dead at the first Passover. Therefore they believed that the second born son needed special protection from the gods and the inscription sought to provide it.

When God dealt with Pharaoh, He first had to inform his mind; then He had to break his will. Pharaoh's problem was not that he did not have sufficient intellectual evidence to believe God and surrender to Him. Instead, his heart had to be broken and made soft towards God. Before Pharaoh asked, *Who is the LORD, that I should obey His voice to let Israel go? I do not know the LORD, nor will I let Israel go* (Exodus 5:2). After his firstborn died on the night of the first Passover, Pharaoh knew who the LORD God was, and he knew that the LORD God was greater than all the Egyptian gods and greater than Pharaoh himself - who was thought to be a god.

What will it take for you to see who God is? Make it easy on yourself. Let your will be broken before His will today, before your will hardens against Him any further.

TWENTY-ONE
Reading from Exodus: Chapter 13

A ROAD THAT IS LONGER, TOUGHER, AND BETTER

Then it came to pass, when Pharaoh had let the people go, that God did not lead them by way of the land of the Philistines, although that was near; for God said, "Lest perhaps the people change their minds when they see war, and return to Egypt." So God led the people around by way of the wilderness of the Red Sea. (Exodus 13:17-18)

Pharaoh finally let go and let the people of Israel leave Egypt. After the terror of the death of the firstborn, Israel couldn't leave soon enough for Pharaoh. He pushed them out. As they left in a long procession out of Egypt, God had a road for them to travel.

In that day travel between Egypt and the empires of the north and west was common, and the roads to these empires led through the area we know today as Israel. There were a few different well maintained and well traveled roads that could take the children of Israel right to the Promised Land. But God didn't want them to take the easy road.

The coastal road was known in the ancient world as the *Via Maris*, which is translated as "the way of the sea." It was the shortest and most common way to go; but it was also the road where Egypt's military outposts were established. God knew the people of Israel were not ready to face this challenge yet, so He led them a different way.

In the same way, God will never allow us to face more than we are able to bear. He knows what we can handle. 1

Corinthians 10:13 says *No temptation has overtaken you except such as is common to man; but God is faithful, who will not allow you to be tempted beyond what you are able, but with the temptation will also make the way of escape, that you may be able to bear it.* God knows what we can bear.

It would have been easy for the Israelites to think that the Via Maris was the way to go. It was a good road and easy to travel on. It made the trip in the shortest distance, and it was a trade route so food and water could be bought along the way. But the dangers of the way by the sea were too great, even though they probably could not see what those dangers were. The same is true of our walk with God; a way that seems right to us may turn out to be full of danger we can't even think of. Think of all the disaster God has kept you from when you couldn't even see the danger. Today, thank God for His goodness, because sometimes the longer and tougher road is also really the better road.

TWENTY-TWO
Reading from Exodus: Chapters 13-14

THE RIGHT KIND OF REBELLION

And the LORD hardened the heart of Pharaoh king of Egypt, and he pursued the children of Israel; and the children of Israel went out with boldness. (Exodus 14:8)

Israel was on its way out of Egypt, and Pharaoh decided that it wasn't a good thing. So he sent against the escaping Israelites the finest military technology in the world at that time: the chariot. 600 chariots bore down on the defenseless children of Israel.

None of that mattered, because Israel had a bold trust in God. Our passage from Exodus makes it clear: **The children of Israel went out with boldness**. Pharaoh had his chariots, but Israel had boldness in their God.

The idea behind the ancient Hebrew words **with boldness** include the idea of rebellion against authority. The same Hebrew words are used just this way in 1 Kings 11:26-27. A Psalm also describes this kind of rebellion on the part of Israel at the Red Sea: *Our fathers in Egypt did not understand Your wonders; they did not remember the multitude of Your mercies, but rebelled by the sea; the Red Sea* (Psalm 106:7-12).

It seems that by nature this generation of Israelites was pretty rebellious. Their rebellious nature was good when it was against Pharaoh and all he stood for. But their rebellious nature was bad when it was directed against the LORD, against Moses, and against all that they stood for.

Is it bad to be a rebel? It depends what you rebel against. If you rebel against the Prince of the Power of the Air (the devil), that's good. If you rebel against the world system that rejects God, that's good. If you rebel against your fleshly nature, that's good. There is a lot of good rebellion that God wants us to enjoy. The trouble with most rebels is that they rebel against the wrong things.

Unfortunately, our rebellion often gets directed against the LORD and the authorities He establishes. On their way to the Promised Land, Israel would show plenty of the bad kind of rebellion. But at the moment described in Exodus 14:8, they showed the good kind of rebellion. Which kind of rebellion is more evident in your life?

TWENTY-THREE
Reading from Exodus: Chapter 14

WHEN PHARAOH DRAWS NEAR

And when Pharaoh drew near...they were very afraid, and the children of Israel cried out to the LORD. Then they said to Moses, "Because there were no graves in Egypt, have you taken us away to die in the wilderness?" (Exodus 14:10-11)

It wasn't easy to leave Egypt. It was a long process but God had a purpose in the process. Through the plagues on Egypt God did something in the heart of Israel. Through the Passover God taught them to trust Him even more. But there was a sense in which Israel's problems didn't even begin until the people of Israel left Egypt. Now on their way out, Pharaoh decided he didn't like the idea after all. He sent his mighty army against defenseless Israel. How did God's people react?

First they reacted with fear: **They were very afraid**. All in all, this made sense. According to everything anyone could see, Israel was in serious trouble. Behind them were Pharaoh's armies. Ahead of them was the Red Sea. There was really no chance for escape.

God doesn't blame us for being afraid when we are in a frightening situation. It is what we do with the fear that matters. It was the LORD Himself who led Israel right into a cul-de-sac. There was no way of escape except the way they came, and the Egyptian army had that way covered.

Second, they reacted with prayer: They **cried out to the LORD**. This was good; when we are in a dangerous position we must cry out to God, because "God is our refuge and strength, a very present help in trouble" (Psalm 46:1). Often we make prayer our last resort, when God wants it to be our first resource. Here, the LORD brought Israel to their last resort in a hurry.

Third, they reacted with panic and unjust accusation. **Then they said to Moses... "Because there were no graves in Egypt, have you taken us away to die in the wilderness?"** Here the children of Israel began to lose it. They thought Moses was motivated by a desire to see all Israel die in the wilderness. Moses said or did nothing that supported such a conspiracy theory, but the children of Israel could still think and say, "this is the real reason he brought us out here." We are often wrong and always on dangerous ground when we claim to read the intentions of other's hearts. Instead of reacting this way, Israel should have said, "Moses this is hard and we are afraid. But we know God has been with you and we trust He is with you now. We'll follow you if you lead us."

Fourth, they reacted with selective memory. **Let us alone that we may serve the Egyptians**. Israel was not yet a week out of Egypt and they already distorted the past, thinking it was better in Egypt than it really was. Already they remembered the "good old days" of Egypt. Instead of reacting this way, Israel should have said, "We remember the hundreds of years of bitter slavery in Egypt, and even though this is tough, it is better than Egypt. We're choosing to trust God."

Perhaps we thought that Satan would let us go easily; or that once we had left his kingdom, he would forget about us. It doesn't work that way. Satan will pursue you, hoping to keep you at least on the fringes of his domain, and he will try to destroy you if he can. Are you ready for the attack? In your life, "when Pharaoh draws near," how will you react? If you are already under attack, are you looking to the past or to the future for refuge?

TWENTY-FOUR
Reading from Exodus: Chapter 14

STAND STILL

*Moses said to the people, "Do not be afraid. Stand still, and
see the salvation of the LORD." (Exodus 14:13)*

It didn't look good. In front of the huge multitude of Israel
was the Red Sea, an impassable body of water. Behind them
was the fast-charging Egyptian army. Right in the middle was
a multitude quickly losing faith in God. At this point, Moses
had no idea how God would come through in the situation.
All he knew was that God would certainly come through. In
a sense, Moses knew he was in such a bad situation that God
had to come through.

When we see that our only help is God we are more likely
to trust Him. Sometimes it is the little things that get us
down, the things we think we can do in our own strength.
In this sense the big problems can be easier, because we know
only God can bring the solution.

Moses looked at the desperate situation, and spoke for the
LORD when he said to Israel, **stand still**. These words are still
often the LORD's direction to the believer in a crisis.

When you are in a crisis, *despair* will try to cast you down
and keep you from standing.

Fear will tell you to retreat instead of standing still.

Impatience will tell you to do something, even anything
now instead of standing still.

Presumption will tell you to jump into the Red Sea before
God parts it with a miracle.

Instead of any of these options, God tells us to **stand**, and to stand **still**.

In Job 37:14, Elihu gave Job good counsel: *Stand still and consider the wondrous works of God.* Are things pressing around you? Are you caught in the middle of impossible circumstances? Then make sure you are standing where God wants you to stand. He wants you to stand on His Word, to stand on His character, and to stand on His promises. Find that place, and then stand still right there.

Put on the whole armor of God, that you may be able to ***stand*** *against the wiles of the devil... Therefore take up the whole armor of God, that you may be able to withstand in the evil day, and having done all, to* ***stand***. (Galatians 5:11, 13)

TWENTY-FIVE
Reading from Exodus: Chapter 14

WHEN IT IS WRONG TO PRAY

And the LORD said to Moses, "Why do you cry to Me? Tell the children of Israel to go forward." (Exodus 14:15)

The situation was desperate. The Egyptian army rushed towards the defenseless people of Israel. There was no where to go except through the impossible – through the watery expanse of the Red Sea right in front of them. Moses did what any one of us might counsel him to do: he prayed. However, it was the wrong thing to do at the time. It wasn't time to pray, it was time to act.

God simply asked Moses, **Why do you cry to Me?** The answer seemed obvious. "LORD, I cry to You because there is nothing else to do. We will be destroyed in a matter of hours unless you do something. Can't you see that is why I cry out to You?" But there is a time to pray, and a time *not* to pray. Moses had his time mixed up.

It might sound strange, but there are times when prayer isn't the right thing to do. Of course, we don't mean the attitude of constant communication we can have with God, thus fulfilling the command to *pray without ceasing* (1 Thessalonians 5:17). Instead, think of the times of separated, "I'm-doing-nothing-else-but-praying-right-now" times of prayer. There are times when that kind of prayer might be wrong. It can actually be against God's will to stop everything and pray in a particular situation.

It is wrong to pray out of the wrong motives. Sometimes we pray selfishly, not only asking things for ourselves (which isn't necessarily wrong), but asking for things to meet our selfish desires and ambitions. Then it is the wrong time to pray, and the LORD could well ask us, **Why do you cry to Me?**

It is wrong to pray with others intending to *inform* those who listen. Some people who think they never gossip actually gossip a great deal in prayer meetings. Instead of talking to God in prayer, they use prayer as a time to tell others gossipy things in a "holy" setting. Then it is the wrong time to pray, and the LORD could well ask us, **Why do you cry to Me?**

It is wrong to pray with the purpose of *controlling* a situation. Some, with just the right touch of holy tremor in their voice, know how to say "Let's pray." Then they pray, talking to man as much as God, hoping to influence others instead of influencing God. Then, it is the wrong time to pray, and the LORD could well ask us, **Why do you cry to Me?**

It is wrong to pray with the purpose of *avoiding action* or buying time. Many, when asked to do something, say "Let me pray about it," and they never pray about it at all. They may think about it or talk to others about it but they don't really pray about it. Or if they do pray they don't really seek God about it. For them, prayer is more of a delaying tactic than seeking the face of God. Then it is the wrong time to pray, and the LORD could well ask us, **Why do you cry to Me?**

It is a testimony to the warped nature we received from Adam that we can take something as good and holy as prayer and use it in a wrong way. May God help us to pray more in the right way, and less in the wrong way.

TWENTY-SIX
Reading from Exodus: Chapters 14-15

A MIRACLE ANY WAY YOU LOOK AT IT

Then Moses stretched out his hand over the sea; and the
LORD caused the sea to go back by a strong east wind all that
night, and made the sea into dry land, and the
waters were divided. (Exodus 14:21)

You've seen it in the movies – either in *The Ten Commandments* or *The Prince of Egypt* or *Exodus: Gods and Kings*. You may have experienced it on the tour tram at the Universal Studios amusement park. But some wonder if it really happened. They wonder if Moses really did stretch out his hand over the sea, and if the sea really did part.

The Hebrew phrase translated "Red Sea" (in most Bibles) are the ancient Hebrew words *yam suph*, which clearly means "Reed Sea" not "Red Sea." It seems that Moses didn't part the huge expanse of the Red Sea, but a small finger of it in the lake region north of the Gulf of Suez. We know this was the approximate area because the Israelites found themselves in the Wilderness of Shur after crossing the sea (Exodus 15:22).

We don't know exactly where the place was, and what the exact geography was. After all, areas like this change geography every flood or drought season. We do know there was enough water there to trap the Israelites, and enough to later drown the Egyptians - perhaps 10 feet (3 meters) or so of water. We also know there had to be enough room for the Israelites to cross over in one night – perhaps a mile wide stretch.

Some people regard this as just another interesting legend, but it is completely plausible, according to a *Los Angeles*

Times article many years ago (March 14, 1992) by Thomas H. Maugh titled "Research Supports Bible's Account of Red Sea Parting." In that article, Maugh wrote:

> Sophisticated computer calculations indicate that the biblical parting of the Red Sea, said to have allowed Moses and the Israelites to escape from bondage in Egypt, could have occurred precisely as the Bible describes it. Because of the peculiar geography of the northern end of the Red Sea, researchers report Sunday in the Bulletin of the American Meteorological Society, a moderate wind blowing constantly for about 10 hours could have caused the sea to recede about a mile and the water level to drop 10 feet, leaving dry land in the area where many biblical scholars believe the crossing occurred.

That's a fine scientific description of what may have happened, and we are thankful for it. But I much prefer God's description, found in Psalm 77:16-20:

> *The waters saw You, O God; the waters saw You, they were afraid; the depths also trembled. The clouds poured out water; the skies sent out a sound; Your arrows also flashed about. The voice of Your thunder was in the whirlwind; the lightnings lit up the world; the earth trembled and shook. Your way was in the sea, Your path in the great waters, and Your footsteps were not known. You led Your people like a flock by the hand of Moses and Aaron.*

It usually isn't bad to analyze God's work, whether His work is in history or in our day-to-day lives. But it should never rob us of the wonder and glory we find in just praising God for His great works, no matter how He chooses to do them. The same miracle-working God who led His people like a flock by the hand of Moses and Aaron is here to lead us also.

TWENTY-SEVEN
Reading from Exodus: Chapter 15

BITTER MADE SWEET

So Moses brought Israel from the Red Sea; then they went out into the Wilderness of Shur. And they went three days in the wilderness and found no water. Now when they came to Marah, they could not drink the waters of Marah, for they were bitter. Therefore the name of it was called Marah. And the people complained against Moses, saying, "What shall we drink?" So he cried out to the LORD, and the LORD showed him a tree. When he cast it into the waters, the waters were made sweet. (Exodus 15:22-25)

The miracle of the Red Sea was spectacular, but three days is time enough to forget the victory. Now Israel faced a long trip through a difficult, dry desert. After three dry and thirsty days they finally came to water. But it seemed like a cruel joke when they found the pool of water. They finally came upon water and found that water undrinkable. The water was bitter so they named the place **Marah** – which means "bitter."

But God had a plan. He directed Moses to take a tree – or perhaps a portion of the tree – and throw it into the polluted pool. Somehow the tree made the waters drinkable, and God supplied their need. Many speculate on how the tree actually worked. Jamie Buckingham (from his book on the Exodus journey) believed that the chemicals in the sap of the broken limb drew the mineral content down to the bottom of the pool, and left only good water on the top where they could drink it.

Buckingham went even further. Based on the mineral composition of water pools in that part of the world, he thought that though the waters were now drinkable, they still would contain a significant magnesium and calcium content. These chemicals would have a laxative effect on the nation of Israel – which would make them uncomfortable for a few days, but Buckingham believed it would effectively purge their bodies from the common Egyptian ailments such as amoebic dysentery and bilharzia, a weakening disease common among Egyptian peasants. In addition, the calcium and magnesium together would form the basis of a drug called dolomite - used by some athletes to enhance performance in hot weather conditions. If Buckingham was correct, then at Marah God provided the right medicine to both clean out their systems and to prepare them for a long, hot journey to Mount Sinai.

One way or another, the point is evident. God wasn't only interested in getting the children of Israel out of Egypt. He also wanted to get Egypt out of the children of Israel - both physically and spiritually. God's plan was to transform a slave people into Promised Land people. He used some tough times in the desert to accomplish that goal but He always kept the goal in sight. His goal wasn't to make them thirsty at Marah, but to make them Promised Land people.

His work is essentially the same in us. That means God has to take us out of a sinful environment and then He must take a sinful environment out of us. Think about what God wants to work out of you today, making you more of a Promised Land person.

TWENTY-EIGHT
Reading from Exodus: Chapter 16

WHAT IS IT?

In the morning the dew lay all around the camp. And when the layer of dew lifted, there, on the surface of the wilderness, was a small round substance, as fine as frost on the ground. So when the children of Israel saw it, they said to one another, "What is it?" For they did not know what it was. And Moses said to them, "This is the bread which the LORD has given you to eat." (Exodus 16:13-15)

They came to call it "manna" (Exodus 16:31), but at first they just wondered what it was. A huge nation traveled through a vast wilderness and they needed food. They couldn't just buy it; they had to trust God to provide it and He sent the supply every morning from heaven.

The bread from heaven came with the dew each morning, as a "residue" from the dew. It was small, round and as fine as frost on the ground. Thus it was not easy to gather. It had to be "swept" up from the ground. Exodus 16:31 further describes the bread from heaven as something like coriander seed (about the size of a sesame seed), and sweet like honey; Numbers 11:7 says it was the color of bdellium (a pearl-like color). Manna was prepared by either baking or boiling (Exodus 16:23).

In trying to exactly identify what this bread from heaven was, many seek to identify it with what the Arabs today call *mann*. According to Buckingham, *mann* is formed when "A tiny insect punctures the bark of the tamarisk tree, drinks the sap, and exudes a clear liquid that solidifies as a sugary globule when it hits the ground. When the sun comes up, it melts quickly and disappears." Perhaps the bread from heaven was similar to the modern *mann* in the Sinai Peninsula, but it wasn't the same thing. The modern *mann* never appears in great quantities, it doesn't last year round, and it is confined to a small geographic region.

Most people want to know what manna was. Yet a better question is, "Why did God feed them with manna?" His purpose in sending the bread from heaven was not only to provide for the material needs of Israel, but to teach them eternal lessons of dependence on God:

So He humbled you, allowed you to hunger, and fed you with manna which you did not know nor did your fathers know, that He might make you know that man shall not live by bread alone; but man lives by every word that proceeds from the mouth of the LORD. (Deuteronomy 8:3)

In our place of need, God wants to do more than only meet the need. He wants to teach eternal lessons. Sometimes God has to teach us this way because we are too thick headed to learn any other way. "When they could not be reached in any other way, they have been instructed by their hunger, and by their thirst, and by their feeding." (Spurgeon)

The sending of manna also taught Israel how to work with God. They couldn't just lay back and ask God to put it into their mouths. Feeding Israel through the bread from heaven was an example of God's way of cooperating with man. Israel *could* not supply the manna and God *would* not gather it for them. Each had to do their part.

When the manna came, Israel didn't know what it was. The name "manna" (given later in Exodus 16:31) meant, "what's that?" It came from the question asked in Exodus 16:15. When God provides we often don't recognize it. God has promised to meet all our needs - not all our expectations. Today, let God do His part while you do your part.

TWENTY-NINE
Reading from Exodus: Chapter 17

HANDS STRETCHED OUT

And so it was, when Moses held up his hand, that Israel prevailed; and when he let down his hand, Amalek prevailed. But Moses' hands became heavy; so they took a stone and put it under him, and he sat on it. And Aaron and Hur supported his hands, one on one side, and the other on the other side; and his hands were steady until the going down of the sun. So Joshua defeated Amalek and his people with the edge of the sword.
(Exodus 17:11-13)

The nomads of Amalek attacked Israel as they went through the wilderness, and they attacked them in the worst way – focusing on the weak and the helpless that were at the back of the huge procession. God ordered Israel to go to war against the Amalekites, and while Joshua led the battle Moses supported the work behind the scenes in prayer. The fate of Israel in battle depended on Moses' intercession. In his early days Moses thought the only way to win a battle was to fight. Now he let Joshua fight, while he did the more important work: to pray for the victory.

When Moses **held up his hand** it meant that he was in the Israelite posture of prayer, even as we might bow our heads and fold our hands. When Moses prayed Israel won; when he stopped praying, Amalek prevailed. How could this be? How could life or death for Israel depend on the prayers of one man? God wants us to pray with this kind of passion, believing that life and death – perhaps eternal life and death – may depend on our prayer.

It can be difficult to reconcile this with knowing God has a pre-ordained plan; but God didn't want Moses to concern himself with that – he was to pray knowing that his prayer really mattered. Just because we can't figure out how our prayers mesh with God's pre-ordained plan never means we should stop believing prayer matters.

Prayer is sometimes sweet and easy; other times it is hard work. This is why Paul described the ministry of Epaphras as *always laboring fervently for you in prayers* (Colossians 4:12), and why Paul wrote we must *continue earnestly in prayer, being vigilant in it with thanksgiving* (Colossians 4:2).

This work of prayer was so important that the job was too big for Moses alone. Aaron and Hur came along side Moses and literally held his hands up in prayer; they helped him and partnered with him in intercession. Though this was Moses' work to do, it was more than he could do by himself; the battle of prayer could not be won by him alone. He needed others to come along side to strengthen and support him in prayer.

Because of this work of prayer, Israel was victorious over Amalek – we are left with no other option than to say if Moses, Aaron, and Hur did not do this work in prayer, the battle would have been lost – and history would be changed. Prayer matters. How many victories are lost because God's people will not pray?

Moses did pray. He prayed with his hands stretched out to God, and the battle was won. When Jesus accomplished the greatest victory over Satan, His hands were also stretched out.

What battle is waiting to be won by your prayers?

THIRTY
Reading from Exodus: Chapters 18-19

ON EAGLES' WINGS

You have seen what I did to the Egyptians, and how I bore you on eagles' wings and brought you to Myself. (Exodus 19:4)

The people of Israel finished the first part of their journey – they came out of Egypt and came to Mount Sinai. Ahead of them was a year at Mount Sinai as God gave them His law. As they arrived at the same mountain where the LORD spoke to Moses out of the burning bush, God had something very special to say to the people of Israel.

First, He reminded them of His triumph over the Egyptians (**You have seen what I did to the Egyptians**). Israel needed to be reminded over and over again that the LORD their God was greater than any of Egypt's pretend deities. In our life, there should never be a competition between God and anything else. We must remember that He is greater than anyone and anything.

Next, He spoke to them about His loving care. In saying, **How I bore you on eagle's wings**, the LORD used a precious and powerful picture. It is said that a mother eagle does not carry her young in her claws like other birds. Instead, the young eagles attach themselves to the back of the mother eagle and are protected from any attack from the ground as they are carried. Any arrow from a hunter must pass through the mother eagle before it can touch the young eagle on her back. The LORD has the same loving care for us. Whatever arrows or attacks come your way must first come through the LORD Himself.

This is true in two ways. First, Jesus endured all temptation while He walked this earth as a man. The Bible says that Jesus *was in all points tempted as we are, yet without sin* (Hebrews 4:15). Enthroned in heaven, at the right hand of God the Father, Jesus understands perfectly the arrow shot at you because the same arrow was shot at Him.

Second, whatever comes our way must come by the allowance of God. God is never the source of evil or temptation, but it is fully within God's power to stop any trial or temptation at any time. The fact that He allowed it means He has a purpose for the difficulty in your life – and the purpose isn't to kill you. His purpose is to transform you into the image of Jesus Christ. God never wastes trials or suffering in our life.

Finally, He spoke to Israel about the purpose of His deliverance. He rescued Israel so they could have a relationship with Him. As He brought them out of Egypt God said, **I brought you to Myself**. God didn't deliver Israel so they could do their own thing, but so they could be God's people. So it is in your life. We were not rescued by Jesus so we could live to ourselves, but that we might live unto Him. As 2 Corinthians 5:15 says it, *He died for all, that those who live should live no longer for themselves, but for Him who died for them and rose again.*

His purpose is to bring us to Himself. Are you living according to His purpose, or are you resisting the purpose of God? He rescued you to be with Him.

THIRTY-ONE
Reading from Exodus: Chapter 19

TWO MOUNTAINS

Then it came to pass on the third day, in the morning, that there were thunderings and lightnings, and a thick cloud on the mountain; and the sound of the trumpet was very loud, so that all the people who were in the camp trembled. And Moses brought the people out of the camp to meet with God, and they stood at the foot of the mountain. Now Mount Sinai was completely in smoke, because the LORD descended upon it in fire. Its smoke ascended like the smoke of a furnace, and the whole mountain quaked greatly. (Exodus 19:16-18)

The people of God came out of Egypt, but were still a long way from the Promised Land. On their way there, God led them to Mount Sinai, where they spent a year receiving God's Law and the plans for a special place to meet with God.

When the LORD appeared to the people at Sinai, it wasn't a pleasant or easy experience for Israel. Remember what they saw and felt: thunder, lightning, thick smoke around the mountain, earthquakes, and the eerie sound of a heavenly trumpet. All this made the people of God tremble and filled them with fear at the holy, awesome presence of God.

Some feel today we need more of the fear of Mount Sinai as a way of keeping people from sin. But all of the fear and trembling of Exodus 19 didn't keep the people of Israel from sin. Not even forty days from this, many of the same people who trembled at God's holy presence had a drunken, immoral party around a golden calf, praising it as the god that brought them out of Egypt. Holding God in awe is one thing; submitting our will to Him is another thing. Israel had plenty of awe, but not much submission of the will.

The New Testament compares the fiery, quaking Mount Sinai of Exodus 19 to a different mountain – Mount Zion, where Jesus died for our sins. Hebrews 12:18-24 tells us loud and clear that we have come to a different mountain, that our salvation and relationship with God is centered at Mount Zion, not Mount Sinai. The writer to the Hebrews made these comparisons:

- Sinai spoke of fear and terror, but Zion speaks of love and forgiveness.

- Sinai, with all its fear and power is earthly; but Zion is heavenly and spiritual.

- At Sinai, Moses alone could come and meet God. At Zion, there is an innumerable company, a general assembly who gets to meet God.

- Sinai had guilty men stricken with fear, but Zion has just men made perfect.

- At Sinai, Moses was the mediator; but at Zion Jesus was the mediator.

- Sinai produced an Old Covenant, ratified by the blood of animals. Zion has a New Covenant, ratified by the blood of God's precious Son.

- Sinai was all about barriers and exclusion, but Zion is all about invitation.

- Sinai was focused on law, Zion is focused on grace.

The application from Hebrews 12 is plain. We shouldn't come to God under the New Covenant (represented by Zion) as if we were coming to God under the Old Covenant (represented by Sinai). None of God's people could come to Sinai with bold, confident expectation. Sinai was all about fear and boundaries. Since we come to Zion instead of Sinai, put away your hesitation and get bold in coming to God. He is ready to meet with you.

THIRTY-TWO
Reading from Exodus: Chapter 20

WHY GOD CAN TELL US WHAT TO DO

And God spoke all these words, saying: "I am the LORD your God, who brought you out of the land of Egypt, out of the house of bondage. You shall have no other gods before Me."
(Exodus 20:1-3)

On the way to the Promised Land, God commanded Israel to live at a mountain named Sinai for a year. God did some important things during that time, and one of the most important things was giving Israel His Law.

The Law of God (you can also call it the Law of Moses), are both much more than the Ten Commandments. But the Ten Commandments are unique and important unto themselves, for two reasons. First, the Ten Commandments communicate the essence and the spirit of the entire Law of Moses. They provide a handy, memorable summary of all the principles behind the Law. Second, the Ten Commandments were spoken to the *entire* nation of Israel by God, directly from heaven. Notice what it says: **And God spoke all these words**. God spoke most of this law first to Moses, and then Moses related it to the rest of the people of Israel. But this was not the case with the Ten Commandments; God spoke them from heaven directly to the entire nation. The Israelites heard these words from the voice of God.

The Ten Commandments were not invented at Sinai. A few aspects of the Law of Moses declared something new, but for the most part it simply clearly and definitely laid out God's law as it was written in the heart of man since the time of Adam. In his book *The Abolition of Man*, C.S. Lewis explained how there is a universal morality among men. He showed how all cultures in the past have been able to agree on the basics of morality because they were implanted in the heart of man. Every human culture we have ever known any thing about has said that murder is wrong and that kindness is good. All cultures have said that we have particular obligations to our family, that honesty is good, that a man cannot have any woman he wants, that stealing is wrong, and that justice is good. There really is a basic, universal code of morality written on the heart of man. After all, where is there a culture where being a coward is good and being brave is bad?

Yet in our modern world, there has been a massive shift, to the point where most reject the idea of moral absolutes, saying that it all depends on the situation. People think if there is *one* case where a lie is justified (say to save a life), then all restraints are off and lies are justified in all sorts of situations – especially in their situation! Our inability to believe in and teach a common morality has crippled our culture morally.

In 1990, media mogul Ted Turner decided that the Ten Commandments were out of date, and thought he could do better. He distributed his "10 Voluntary Initiatives" and hoped they would replace the Ten Commandments. This is traveling a great distance, but it is hard to call it progress.

Before God commanded anything of man, He declared who He was: **I am the LORD your God**. Before any command, He declared what He did; that He was the one **who brought you out of the land of Egypt, out of the house of bondage**. There was a real connection: because of who God is and what He did for us, He has the right to tell us what to do – and we have the obligation to obey Him. If you think about who God is, and what He did for you, then it will be a lot easier for you to do what He asks of you today. Try it for yourself and see.

THIRTY-THREE
Reading from Exodus: Chapters 20-21

FEAR AND LOVE

Then they said to Moses, "You speak with us, and we will
hear; but let not God speak with us, lest we die."
(Exodus 20:19)

The people of Israel assembled at the foot of Mount
Sinai and they heard the Lord's own voice declare the Ten
Commandments. We might have thought they would be on a
"spiritual high" after such an experience, but just the opposite
was true. They were terrified. In a sense, this was exactly what
God wanted. Israel knew just how far they fell short of the
glory of their great God. They knew from both the content
of the law and the display of God's glory that the Lord was
perfect and holy and they were not.

Later in Israel's history, they worked to reinterpret the
Law so it wasn't scary anymore. Changing the heart and
intent of the Law, they molded it so it was easy to keep, to
the point where Saul of Tarsus wrote of himself, *concerning*
the righteousness which is in the law, [I was counted] *blameless*
(Philippians 3:6).

In their fear and dread they did not want God to speak to
them anymore, as He spoke the Ten Commandments from
Mount Sinai. Instead, they wanted Moses to stand between
them and God as a mediator. Their instinctive desire for a
mediator was good, because they needed one. But man's
desire for a mediator – someone to act as a go-between with
us and God - is only good if it is fulfilled in Jesus Christ, *for*
there is one God and one Mediator between God and men, the

Man Christ Jesus (1 Timothy 2:5). Unfortunately, some who are aware of their need for a mediator look to someone other than Jesus - and end in ruin.

Their fear at Mount Sinai did not do them much good. Fear can keep us from sin for a while, but fear's power will usually fade over time. The fear Israel experienced at Mount Sinai faded enough in forty days so that they danced around a golden calf, proclaiming it as the God that brought them out of Egypt.

Though it is better to obey God out of fear than to disobey Him, the ultimate motivation for obedience is love: "There is no fear in love; but perfect love casts out fear, because fear involves torment. But he who fears has not been made perfect in love. *We love Him because He first loved us* (1 John 4:18-19). Spend some time today letting God love you, then use your gratitude to walk right before Him.

THIRTY-FOUR
Reading from Exodus: Chapters 22-23

A PREPARED PLACE

*Behold, I send an Angel before you to keep you in the way
and to bring you into the place which I have prepared. Beware
of Him and obey His voice; do not provoke Him, for He
will not pardon your transgressions; for My name is in Him.*
(Exodus 23:20-21)

Moses received the Law from God and brought it down from Mount Sinai to the people of Israel. Now God looked ahead to their journey into the Promised Land. Israel had the Law, but the Law alone could never bring them into the place of rest and blessing the Promised Land was meant to be. They needed a *person* to bring them in, and that person was **an Angel before you to keep you in the way and to bring you into the place which I have prepared**.

This was one special **Angel**. This Angel would keep Israel in the right path. This Angel would lead Israel into the Promised Land. This Angel would command the obedience of Israel. This Angel had the authority to forgive or retain sins. This Angel had the name of God in His own Person. Who was this special Angel?

We only know a few angels by name. Jude 1:9 mentions Michael and Luke 1:19 mentions Gabriel. There is a sense in which each of these have the name of God "in" them. The generic Hebrew word for God is "El" and these two are named Micha-el and Gabri-el, each having the name of God in their name.

But neither Michael or Gabriel could command obedience from Israel or presume to sit in judgment over them. This was the specific Angel of the Lord, Jesus appearing in the Old Testament, before His incarnation in Bethlehem who often speaks directly as the Lord. The name Yahweh is in Jesus. His name is literally Yah-shua – "The Lord is salvation." It shouldn't confuse us that Jesus is occasionally called an Angel, because the word "angel" literally means *a messenger*.

Jesus is much more than a messenger, but He certainly was heaven's ultimate Messenger. When we say Jesus was an Angel, we don't mean that He is or was an angelic being, like other angels described in the Bible. We mean that He has a unique role as heaven's most special messenger.

Since this Angel was Jesus, it means that Jesus was with Israel in all their wilderness experience. It means that Jesus brought them into the Promised Land. It means that Jesus was the One to be obeyed. It means that Jesus had the power to forgive or retain sins. Jesus was each of these things for ancient Israel in the wilderness, and He is also those things for us today.

The Angel went before them **into the place which I have prepared**. Not only is it true that Jesus goes before us to prepare a place for us in heaven (John 14:2-3), but the place you walk in today was prepared by God. Where you will walk tomorrow is also prepared by Him. If you are worried about today or about tomorrow, then put yourself into Jesus by faith and trust, and He will make sure you are in a place prepared by Him.

THIRTY-FIVE
Reading from Exodus: Chapter 24

TERMS OF THE CONTRACT

And Moses wrote all the words of the LORD...[they] offered burnt offerings and sacrificed peace offerings of oxen to the LORD.... Then he took the Book of the Covenant and read in the hearing of the people. And they said, "All that the LORD has said we will do, and be obedient." And Moses took the blood, sprinkled it on the people, and said, "This is the blood of the covenant which the LORD has made with you according to all these words." (Exodus 24:4-8)

A contract brings together two or more parties in binding agreement, according to certain terms. This idea is familiar in the Bible, except that in the Bible contracts are typically called "covenants." Exodus 24 tells us of the "signing ceremony" for the contract God made with Israel. Israel verbally agreed to the covenant-relationship with God (Exodus 24:3) but there was a sense in which this was simply not good enough. They had to do specific things to confirm their covenant with God. Then and now a contract could be considered valid even if it was only a verbal contract. Yet there was often a signing ceremony to reinforce the importance of the covenant. Exodus 24:4-8 tells us about the signing ceremony.

First, the word of God had to be written: **Moses wrote all the words of the LORD.** God's word was important enough that it could not be left up to human recollection and the creative nature of memory. It had to be written down. As it says in Habakkuk 2:2, *Write the vision and make it plain on tablets, that he may run who reads it.*

Second, a covenant was only made with sacrifice. **They offered burnt offerings and sacrificed peace offerings of oxen to the LORD**. They admitted their sin and failing before God, and addressed it through the death of a substitute.

Third, covenant was made when God's word was heard and responded to: **he took the Book of the Covenant and read in the hearing of the people**. This covenant with God was based on His words and His terms, not on the words and terms of men. Additionally, there had to be a response to God's word. The people answered, **All that the LORD has said we will do, and be obedient**. Just as much as God would not negotiate His covenant with Israel, neither would He force it upon them. They had to freely receive it.

Fourth, covenant was made with the application of blood: **Moses took the blood, sprinkled it on the people**. As the nation received the blood of the covenant, the covenant was sealed. It wasn't that there was a magical quality in the blood, but the spilled blood represented the outpouring of life (Leviticus 17:11). It showed one life given for another. Almost a thousand years later God did not forget the blood of this covenant (Zechariah 9:11).

The only way to have a relationship with God is through covenant. He made the terms of a new contract available to us in Jesus. The night before Jesus died on the cross, He explained how the blood of His covenant saves us: *This is My blood of the new covenant, which is shed for many for the remission of sins* (Matthew 26:28). We don't have a relationship with God based on the old covenant, but only on the new covenant – made because of what Jesus did on the cross.

We can't make our own deal with God. We can only receive the covenant He gives us in Jesus. Let that be good enough for you. Thank God for the word of the covenant, the sacrifice of the covenant, the response to the covenant, and the blood of the covenant that rescues you.

THIRTY-SIX
Reading from Exodus: Chapter 25

ACCORDING TO PATTERN

Let them make Me a sanctuary, that I may dwell among them. According to all that I show you, that is, the pattern of the tabernacle and the pattern of all its furnishings, just so you shall make it. (Exodus 25:8-9)

The people of Israel made a remarkable journey out of slavery in Egypt and were on their way to the Promised Land of Canaan. But God never intended for them to enter into the Land of Promise directly. He appointed a year on the way, a year to stay at Mount Sinai. In that year they received the Law and sealed a covenant with God. But that wasn't all. God also intended for Moses to come up on Mount Sinai and receive from God blueprints for a special building.

The building was really a tent, and in Exodus 25:8 God called it a **sanctuary**. It was a special place for the nation of Israel to meet with God through sacrifice and the ministry of the priests. Significantly, God just didn't leave it up to Moses or the architects of Israel to come up with a design. He gave them a pattern for the tabernacle and a pattern for all its furnishings.

God had a specific purpose in the design of the tabernacle. The pattern of the tabernacle was according to a heavenly reality. Hebrews 8:5 tells us that it was a *copy and shadow of the heavenly things*. It therefore had to be made according to exact dimensions, being somewhat of a "model" of God's throne. God wanted the tabernacle to represent a heavenly reality.

Most of the rest of the Book of Exodus deals with the plan and the building of this tent of meeting. To begin with, it is worth noticing how God wanted it to be built. God called Moses up to the mountain, and revealed the plan to the leader of Israel. God said clearly to Moses that he was to make sure the tabernacle was built **according to...the pattern which you were shown on the mountain**. For emphasis, this phrase was repeated in Exodus 26:30, 25:9, and 25:40. The phrase suggests that Moses was actually given a vision of exactly how the tabernacle should look – a vision he had to communicate to the craftsmen who did the actual construction.

God works the same way in leaders today. He gives them a vision of what His work should be and He expects those with the vision to pass it on to others who will do much of the actual work. That means there was a responsibility on both sides. Moses had the responsibility to speak up about what God had shown him, or the work would never get done. The craftsmen had the responsibility to listen to Moses, and to work under his direction.

If God has given you a place of leadership you have a special responsibility to listen to His leading and pass it on to others. If God has put you under a leader, then do what you can to help that leader carry out the direction the LORD gave them. That's how the work of God gets done.

THIRTY-SEVEN
Reading from Exodus: Chapter 25

MORE THAN JUST A BOX

And they shall make an ark of acacia wood; two and a half cubits shall be its length, a cubit and a half its width, and a cubit and a half its height. And you shall overlay it with pure gold, inside and out you shall overlay it, and shall make on it a molding of gold all around. (Exodus 25:10-11)

It was only a wooden box, less than four feet long (one and one-third meters) and three feet wide (one meter). It was covered with gold and had a special golden lid with an ornate sculptured design of angels. It didn't have handles and was never intended to be carried by lifting directly with the hands of a men. Instead it was meant to be carried by inserting gold-overlaid poles into gold rings at each corner of the Ark. Those poles were to stay in the rings, and apart from touching the poles, it was forbidden to touch the Ark of the Covenant.

In 2 Samuel 6:6-7, a man named Uzzah touched the Ark to keep it from falling off a cart, but he did not touch it at the poles and God struck him dead. Uzzah was wrong in thinking that God would let the Ark be damaged; in fact, it did not fall off the cart, and no thanks to Uzzah. Uzzah was also wrong in thinking that there was something less pure about the ground than his act of pure disobedience.

If the Ark of the Covenant was basically a box, we should take note of what was inside of it. Exodus 25 tells us how God told Moses to put "the Testimony" – that is, a copy of the law - into the Ark of the Covenant. Later, God instructed Israel to put other things in the Ark also – things like *the golden pot that had the manna, Aaron's rod that budded, and the tablets of the covenant* (Hebrews 9:4).

The box itself was important, but the lid to the box was worthy of special notice – the lid is called the *mercy seat* in Exodus 25. The mercy seat was made of pure gold and surrounded by artistic interpretations of cherubim. In the picture provided by the Ark of the Covenant, it was as if God dwelt between the two cherubim and met with His people there. The mercy seat was also the place where atoning blood from animal sacrifices was sprinkled (Leviticus 16:14-15). It was as if God looked down from His dwelling place between the cherubim, saw the tablets of the law in the Ark – and knew His people were guilty of breaking His law. But the atoning blood of sacrifice was sprinkled on the mercy seat, so that God saw the blood as it covered over His broken law – and forgiveness could be offered.

In Romans 3:25, the Apostle Paul called Jesus our *propitiation* which was also a word used among early Christians for this same mercy seat. From the way Paul wrote, it might be said "Jesus is our mercy seat" – He is the place and the way of our redemption. In some way, everything in the tabernacle points us to Jesus and His work on our behalf. Remember that you can't provide your own place and way of redemption – Jesus is the place and the way, and God invites you to come.

THIRTY-EIGHT
Reading from Exodus: Chapter 25

FRESH BREAD IS ALWAYS BETTER

You shall also make a table of acacia wood; two cubits shall be its length, a cubit its width, and a cubit and a half its height. And you shall overlay it with pure gold, and make a molding of gold all around... And you shall set the showbread on the table before Me always. (Exodus 25:23-24, 30)

Before Israel left Egypt, Moses knew God wanted him to lead Israel to the Promised Land. He didn't know God also wanted him to be a building supervisor and furniture maker. God commanded Moses to supervise the construction of a special tent where they would meet God, and to build special furnishings for the tent. Both the tent (also known as the "tabernacle") and the furnishings were built after a specific pattern God gave to Moses on Mount Sinai.

One piece of furniture was known as the *Table of Showbread*. We read of its dimensions – about three feet long (one meter), a foot and a half wide (half a meter), and a little more than two feet tall (two-thirds a meter). It was about the size of a tall coffee table, made of acacia wood and overlaid with gold. But the most important thing was not the *Table of Showbread* itself, but the bread that set on it.

As one entered the tabernacle, the *Table of Showbread* stood on the right hand side. It was opposite a golden lampstand holding seven oil lamps that provided the only light for the tent. On this table were twelve loaves of bread – but we would call them cakes, because they were flat. This was the **showbread**, made of fine flour. The twelve cakes of showbread – one for each tribe of Israel - set on the table, sprinkled lightly with frankincense. Once a week the priest put out fresh bread and the priests were allowed to eat the old bread (Leviticus 24:5-9).

It might seem strange for God to set a bakery rack in His holy tabernacle, but there was an important reason for it. The meaning and importance of the showbread is found in the name. Literally, **showbread** means "bread of faces." It was bread associated with, and to be eaten before, the face of God. F.B. Meyer called the showbread "presence-bread." To eat the showbread was to eat God's bread in God's house as a friend and a guest of the LORD, enjoying His hospitality.

In that culture, eating together made a permanent and sacred bond of friendship. Eating the bread in God's house powerfully said, "LORD I love You and seek Your face. I'm in Your presence, seeking transformation by seeing Your face."

The showbread always had to be fresh. On a regular routine the priests took the old showbread, *which had been taken from before the LORD, in order to put hot bread in its place* (1 Samuel 21:6). God wants our fellowship with Him - our time before His face – to be fresh. Your time with God should be freshness dated. Don't be satisfied with a stale, moldy relationship with the LORD.

Everything in the tabernacle pointed to Jesus in one way or another. Jesus identified Himself with the showbread when He said, *I am the bread of life.... This is the bread which comes down from heaven, that one may eat of it and not die. I am the living bread which came down from heaven* (John 6:48-51). As much as we need to eat bread to survive, we need Jesus to live both now and for eternity. We must totally depend on Jesus just as we depend on food. As bread is necessary for survival, so fellowship with God is necessary for man. Today, enjoy some daily bread – some *fresh* bread – from God.

THIRTY-NINE
Reading from Exodus: Chapter 25

THE ONLY REAL LIGHT

You shall also make a lampstand of pure gold; the lampstand shall be of hammered work. And six branches shall come out of its sides: three branches of the lampstand out of one side, and three branches of the lampstand out of the other side... And see to it that you make them according to the pattern which was shown you on the mountain. (Exodus 25:31-32, 40)

The tent God told Moses to build in the wilderness had no windows, so the only light source was what we would call today a menorah. It looked like a seven-branched candlestick, but there were no candles. On top of each branch was a small bowl to hold oil that fueled lamps. Their flickering light chased the darkness from the tent, and the lamps were to be kept burning continually.

God said to hammer the lampstand out of pure gold, and the top of each branch was sculpted in an almond blossom motif. The almond was a special figure because it was the first tree to blossom in springtime.

In Israel today there is a group known as the Temple Mount Faithful who are committed to rebuilding the Jewish temple in Jerusalem, which was simply a permanent version of the tabernacle. In the past several years they made another step towards restoring temple rituals. It remains to be seen if this recently made menorah will stand in a rebuilt temple. But there is no doubt that it is a deliberate connection to this lampstand that God told Moses to make according to the pattern shown to him on the mountain.

This seven-branched lampstand has become an enduring symbol of Israel and the Jewish people. One of the earliest symbols representing the Jewish people unearthed by archaeologists are carvings of this lampstand. On the famous Arch of Titus in Rome, carvings commemorate Rome's victory over Jerusalem in AD 70. In those carvings, the seven-branched lampstand is clearly seen as part of the plunder the Romans took from Jerusalem and paraded into Rome.

Being the only source of light for the tabernacle, the lampstand illuminated everything else in the tent. Entering the tabernacle, eyes were immediately drawn to this golden sculpture. Everything in the tabernacle referred to Jesus in some way, and the lampstand was no exception. Jesus said, *I am the light of the world. He who follows Me shall not walk in darkness, but have the light of life* (John 8:12).

Jesus lights up everything in our dark world, and without Him, nothing else can be seen for what it is. Ideally, our eyes are immediately drawn to Jesus, and He is a continual source of light for us. Let His light be your guide today.

FORTY
Reading from Exodus: Chapter 26

FROM THE INSIDE OUT

Moreover you shall make the tabernacle with ten curtains of fine woven linen and blue, purple, and scarlet thread; with artistic designs of cherubim you shall weave them.
(Exodus 26:1)

When Moses met God on Mount Sinai, he came down with more than the tablets of the law. He also came down with something like blueprints for a special tent God told him to build. It was called the "tent of meeting" or the "tabernacle of God." A **tabernacle** is simply a tent, but this was no ordinary tent – it was the mobile house of God.

Exodus 25 tells us how God told Moses to build three important pieces of furniture for inside the tent. The first was the Ark of the Covenant, which is known to many who have never read the Book of Exodus through the movie *Raiders of the Lost Ark*. The second was the table of showbread, and the third was the golden menorah that gave light to the tent. After describing these three pieces belonging to the inside of the tent, now in Exodus 26, God gives Moses the blueprint for building the tent itself – the exterior of the structure.

There were to be four layers of material covering the tent. The first layer was of fine woven linen, with the artistic design of cherubim. This was the inside layer, which the priests saw inside the tabernacle, reminding them that this represented the throne room of God in heaven. The second layer was a large goat's hair blanket, the third a covering made of ram's skin dyed red, and the fourth and outside layer was of badger skins sewed together in a large leather tarp. These large coverings lay over a system of boards set on silver bases, covered with gold, and connected by gold covered wood rods.

When these four layers of curtains were set on one another, the result was a tent that was very dry and very dark – the only light came from the golden menorah described in the previous chapter. It was in this tent that the priests performed their duties before the LORD.

Much can be said about each particular aspect of the tent itself. The colors, the fabrics, the metals, the way the structure tied together – each of these had an important significance. But there is value in looking at the broader picture – just how the plans for the tabernacle were revealed to Moses. God started from the inside, telling Moses what to put in the tent. Then God worked outwards from there and told Moses how to build the outside. Even in His description of the four coverings, God started from the inside and worked out.

This is how the work of God is always done in our life: from the inside out. First He makes us new men and women in Jesus Christ and lifts us up to sit in heavenly places with Him. That inner work done, He works on the outside. Today, spend some time allowing the LORD to work on the inside – and see what a difference it makes on the outside.

FORTY-ONE
Reading from Exodus: Chapters 27-29

STARTING AND FINISHING

*Now when the people saw that Moses delayed coming down
from the mountain, the people gathered together to Aaron, and
said to him, "Come, make us gods that shall go before us; for as
for this Moses, the man who brought us up out of the land of
Egypt, we do not know what has become of him."*
(Exodus 32:1)

Moses was up on Mount Sinai and he received the plans
for the tabernacle. As the people of Israel waited for him,
they became impatient. The people were troubled because
Moses delayed coming down from the mountain. God had
a wonderful purpose for Moses' delay, and the delay would
soon be over. Yet because the people couldn't see the reason
for the delay, they allowed it to stumble them. Moses was
gone for 40 days (Exodus 24:18). This probably seemed like
a long time for the people, but a short time for Moses. Moses
was up on the mountain in wonderful communication with
God, so he was in no hurry. And God was not in a hurry,
because this was certainly a short time in the outworking of
God's big plan for Israel.

This is a wonderful measure of our spiritual maturity:
how do we handle God's delays? Do we drift off into sin? Do
we give up, resigned to fate instead of trusting in God? God
wants us to receive His delays with a living faith in the living
God. Sadly, Israel didn't live up to this. Soon they worshipped
a statue of a golden calf that the high priest Aaron made for
them. But this sinful impulse came first from the people, not
Aaron. There was a golden calf because the people wanted

one. In this case, giving the people what they wanted was a dangerous thing. This shows why it is wrong to start with what people *want* when we plan ministry or work as a church. The people may very well want a golden calf.

Read what the people said next: **Come, make us gods that shall go before us**. They wanted gods to **go before** them. Where did they want to go? Undoubtedly, they wanted to go to the Promised Land. Israel knew the LORD God led them out of Egypt and they knew the LORD God had revealed Himself at Mount Sinai. Yet, they were willing to trust a false god - a god of their own creation – to finish what they knew the LORD started.

The apostle Paul dealt with the same error with the Galatians: *Are you so foolish? Having begun in the Spirit, are you now being made perfect by the flesh?* (Galatians 3:3) To our shame, some of us trusted in Jesus *more* back when we first came to know Him - now we trust more in our own spiritual ability.

Finally, the people said, **We do not know what has become of him**, referring to Moses. This is a great example of doing something in the flesh simply because **we do not know**. We take on a lot of bitterness or hurt because we assume we know when we do not. Our ignorance should make us turn to God and rely on Him – not the senses and abilities of the flesh.

Today, decide to trust God more as time goes on, instead of trusting Him less. Decide to believe Him *more* when you don't know what is going on, instead of believing Him *less*.

FORTY-TWO
Reading from Exodus: Chapters 30-32

THE REAL GOD OR THE GOD WE MAKE?

And Aaron said to them, "Break off the golden earrings
which are in the ears of your wives, your sons, and your
daughters, and bring them to me." So all the people broke off
the golden earrings which were in their ears, and brought them
to Aaron. And he received the gold from their hand, and he
fashioned it with an engraving tool, and made a molded calf.
Then they said, "This is your god, O Israel, that brought you out
of the land of Egypt!" (Exodus 32:2-4)

The people of Israel decided Moses was gone too long,
up on Mount Sinai listening to the LORD. They wanted to
get moving towards the Promised Land, and because Moses
didn't come down soon enough, they fashioned their own
god to lead them. They came to the high priest Aaron and
asked him to make their god and he was happy to "help."

First Aaron took an offering. **Break off the golden
earrings...and bring them to me**. Before this, God told
Moses how to receive an offering to fund the building of a holy
place for the LORD (Exodus 25:1-7). Here Aaron conducted
an ungodly imitation of that offering – he took a collection
of gold to make an idol. The people responded generously:
**all the people broke off the golden earrings...and brought
them to Aaron**. Sometimes we are more generous with what
we give to ungodly things than with what we give to the
things of God.

Look at what Aaron did once he had the gold: **He
fashioned it with an engraving tool**. This wasn't the Spirit-

inspired craftsmanship of Bezaleel and Aholiab that would later build the tabernacle, but it was the flesh-inspired work of Aaron. He planned it, melted the gold, molded it, and fashioned it carefully with an engraving tool. It didn't just happen. Aaron put work into it. Aaron didn't initiate this idolatry, but he put significant energy into carrying it out.

Then they said, "This is your god." Aaron did not anoint this statue as their god; the people did. Aaron simply went along with the people when they called it **god**. No doubt he was flattered at their admiration of his handiwork. True leadership would have compelled Aaron to cry out, "This is idolatry! We must destroy this. You people are wrong in calling this golden statue your god." But Aaron wasn't a true leader here; he was the type who leads by following popular opinion. Years ago in France, a political mob marched down the street, followed by a running man, who was heard to shout, "Let me through, I have to follow them, I am their leader!" This was Aaron's style of leadership – the wrong style.

Aaron's leadership – or lack of it – lead the people into foolishness. Look at what they said of this statue from Aaron's workshop: **That brought you out of the land of Egypt**. This was madness – to say that this golden calf represented the god that brought them out of Egypt. When we leave the wisdom of following the true God, we can easily fall for the most foolish things. Someone once said, "In the beginning, God made man in His own image, and man has been returning the favor ever since." It's a common trap to fall into.

Are you worshipping a god of your own creation? Nothing is more important than *letting the Bible* tell us who God is, instead of fashioning our own version of "god" in our mind. We can do the opposite of Aaron, leading people to the true God – the God of the Bible – instead of the god of human creation. Ask God for the opportunity to tell someone about the true God, the God who is really there.

FORTY-THREE
Reading from Exodus: Chapter 32

A GOOD TIME BEFORE A FALSE GOD

So when Aaron saw it, he built an altar before it. And Aaron made a proclamation and said, "Tomorrow is a feast to the LORD." Then they rose early on the next day, offered burnt offerings, and brought peace offerings; and the people sat down to eat and drink, and rose up to play. (Exodus 32:5-6)

A funny thing happened on the way to the Promised Land. While Moses was up on Mount Sinai, the people became tired of waiting for Moses and the LORD. So they decided to make their own god. They gave generously to the high priest Aaron and he shaped a golden calf so the people had an object to focus on in their idolatry.

All of that was bad enough; but as events unfolded, it only became worse. It became worse **when Aaron saw it**. When he saw how the people responded to the golden calf, he knew he had something very popular. It was clear that this was a marketing success and they admired Aaron's handiwork. What else could he do, except build an altar before it? They started by giving this statue the credit for their deliverance from Egypt; but now, Aaron felt he had to sanctify the idol with animal sacrifice. He made the calf and then he made the altar to worship it.

Aaron said next, **tomorrow is a feast to the LORD**. After all, Aaron didn't want to reject the LORD. He wanted to give God a feast, so perhaps God wouldn't be mad at them. Aaron was not bold enough to say, "Let's do away with the LORD God." He was just updating things – making things more modern. In Aaron's mind, he *added* the golden calf, he didn't *take away* the God of Israel.

Look at how the people responded to Aaron's offer: **they rose early the next day**. Nobody really likes to get up early, but these ancient Israelites were willing to sacrifice their time, their sleep, their gold, their animals, and even their souls in their worship of this false god. But worshipping an idol isn't all sacrifice. There is a reward – the pleasure of immorality. Exodus tells us that in their worship of the golden calf, they **rose up to play**. In the original language, this is a tasteful way to refer to dark immorality among the people of Israel. After all, golden calves don't have high standards.

Do not forget that this was the same group of people who, 40 days earlier, heard the voice of God Himself thunder from heaven, giving them the Ten Commandments. That dramatic experience, in and of itself, could not change their hearts. It made many of them wish for a less demanding god – a god they could make with their own hands, a god they could give just what they *wanted* to give, and a god they could honor with immorality.

This reflects an enduring spiritual principle: people will always sacrifice for their god. For what, or for whom, will you make a sacrifice? Will you sacrifice for success? Fame? Happiness? Relationships? Whatever or whomever you will sacrifice the most for, that is your god. Indeed, if you will not sacrifice for the Lord, then He is not your God at all. This is a measure of our heart. Can people look at your sacrifices, and see what or Whom you worship?

FORTY-FOUR
Reading from Exodus: Chapter 32

HE SEES IT ALL

And the LORD said to Moses, "Go, get down! For your people whom you brought out of the land of Egypt have corrupted themselves. They have turned aside quickly out of the way which I commanded them. They have made themselves a molded calf, and worshipped it and sacrificed to it, and said, 'This is your god, O Israel, that brought you out of the land of Egypt!'"
(Exodus 32:7-8)

Moses was up on Mount Sinai. The people of Israel waited at the foot of the mountain for Moses to return. While they waited they convinced Aaron, the brother of Moses, to make a golden calf to worship. Aaron obliged and their idolatrous worship soon turned immoral.

Meanwhile, Moses was still with God on Mount Sinai. Moses didn't have any reason to think things went wrong down below. After all, he left Aaron in charge. But things did go wrong, and though Moses didn't know it, God did.

First, there was a distance between God and His people. **For your people whom you brought out of the land of Egypt**. Did you notice the words **your people and whom you brought?** God said to Moses, "these are your people and not Mine." It wasn't that God hated Israel, or even that He had distanced Himself from them. The truth was that Israel moved away from God and moved towards a golden calf. *They* created the distance; God simply recognized it.

There's an old story about an elderly husband and wife driving down the road, sitting on opposite ends of the front bench seat of their car. As they drove, the wife noticed the cars coming the other way had a lot of couples who were snuggled close together, and she said to her husband, "Do you remember when we use to sit close together like that? Why don't we do that any more?" After a thoughtful pause, the elderly man just drove on and said, "I didn't move." Whenever we are far from God, guess who moved?

Next, God knew how **quickly** they turned away from Him. He told Moses that they **turned aside quickly**. That was almost an understatement. They didn't wait long to go their own fleshly way. A few wrong choices can lead us into a bad place in a hurry. Many people fall away gradually, but that isn't always the case. Be on guard against the sudden slide away from God.

Finally, we notice that God described to Moses everything that happened, and He even quoted the words of the people in their idolatry. He heard it when they said, **this is your god, O Israel, that brought you out of the land of Egypt!** God knew exactly what went on. The people ignored God, but He didn't ignore them.

Remember today that God is with you in everything you do. Nothing is hidden from Him. Is that a comfort or a curse to you?

FORTY-FIVE
Reading from Exodus: Chapters 32-33

RELENTING, REPENTING, AND CONTRADICTIONS

So the LORD relented from the harm which He said He would do to His people. (Exodus 32:14)

As Moses received special instructions from God, Israel was in deep rebellion against God. The LORD told Moses all about Israel's disobedience, and how He intended to judge them. Basically, God suggested to Moses that He wipe out the nation and start all over again with Moses. This brought Moses into fervent prayer, and he pled for God's mercy towards the people. God relented, and the nation was saved.

The events themselves are simple enough. But this verse from Exodus 32 is an example of what some consider "problem passages" in the Bible. This is especially true when we read the King James Version, where this verse is translated *the LORD repented of the evil which he thought to do unto his people.* So here is the problem. Does God need to repent of evil? Did God change His mind?

It's useful to look at the work of other translators. Though this work uses the New King James Version, there are also other good translations out there one can use. Here is this passage in some other well-known translations:

Then the LORD relented. (New International Version)

So the LORD changed His mind about the harm which He said He would do to His people. (New American Standard)

The LORD turned from the evil which He had thought to do. (The Amplified Bible)

Reading these other translations is interesting, but it really doesn't solve the "problem" of the verse. After all, Numbers 23:19 says, *God is not a man, that He should lie, nor a son of man, that He should repent.* How then can Moses say that God changed His mind?

We find the answer in understanding that Moses wrote in what we call anthropomorphic, or "man-centered" language. He described the actions of God as they *appeared*. Moses' prayer did not change God, but it did change the standing of the people in God's sight – the people were now in a place of mercy when before they were in a place of judgment.

Yet we can still say that God did not go back on His word. God's promises of judgment are inherently intended to call men to repentance and prayer and therefore be spared the judgment. Ezekiel 33:13-16 is a passage that beautifully describes this truth about God's judgment.

Some are frustrated because the Bible describes God's actions in human terms, but how else could they be described? After all, in what other terms can we speak of God? To speak of God after the manner of God is reserved for God Himself. Even if Moses could write it, we couldn't understand it. In this sense, the LORD often speaks not according to the literal fact, but according to the way things appear to us, so that we may understand as much as humans *can* understand the divine. We take the Bible literally – that is, according to its literary context. When it uses figures of speech and human-centered word pictures, we understand it that way.

When we read a passage like this, it should bring forth at least three reactions. First, we should thank God that there are no contradictions in His Word. Second, we should thank God that He gave us His Word using terms we can understand. Finally, we should thank God that He spares us from the harm we deserve from Him and He relents when we receive by faith what Jesus did to make us right before God.

FORTY-SIX
Reading from Exodus: Chapter 33

SHOW ME THE GLORY

And he said, "Please, show me Your glory." (Exodus 33:18)

Moses had faithfully interceded for the nation of Israel. They deserved the judgment of death, but God spared Israel because Moses prayed. After this Moses had a greater longing – to see the glory of God. At what he sensed was his first opportunity, he asked God, **Please, show me Your glory**. It may have been a soft whisper, and perhaps Moses was almost embarrassed to make such a bold request. But he said it and God heard it.

Show me Your glory is an interesting request. The Bible tells us clearly that Moses had already seen *something* of the glory of God. Exodus 16:10 says *the glory of the* LORD *appeared in the cloud*, and Moses was there to see it. Exodus 24:16-17 says *The glory of the* LORD *rested on Mount Sinai, and the cloud covered it six days. And on the seventh day He called to Moses out of the midst of the cloud*. Moses went up to Mount Sinai in the very midst of that cloud of glory.

Moses saw something of the glory of God, yet knew he hadn't seen anything yet. Maybe he wasn't satisfied with what he already saw. Moses had a hunger for God that could not be filled with a single experience, no matter how wonderful that one experience was. The more of God Moses experienced, the more of God he longed for.

When we really value something, we approach it the same way. A professional baseball player is never satisfied with hitting *one* home run. Lovers are never long satisfied with just *one* kiss. A salesman is never satisfied with just *one* big sale. When we really love something, we quite rightly are not satisfied with just a bit. We want more.

Does that describe how your heart is towards God? Are you easily satisfied in your pursuit of God? Some people only really think of God about two times a year – Christmas and Easter. It shows that they really don't value and love God all that much, because their "hunger" is so easily satisfied.

Jesus said, *Blessed are those who hunger and thirst for righteousness, for they shall be filled* (Matthew 5:6). When we have this kind of hunger for God and His righteousness, He never sees it as being selfish. He sees it as a proper hunger that should be filled.

Spiritually speaking, what are you hungry for? Ask God to give you a deeper hunger for Him, and ask Him to show you how to have that hunger satisfied yet deepened every day.

FORTY-SEVEN
Reading from Exodus: Chapter 34

THE SAME GOD, OLD AND NEW

And the LORD passed before him and proclaimed, "The LORD, the LORD God, merciful and gracious, longsuffering, and abounding in goodness and truth, keeping mercy for thousands, forgiving iniquity and transgression and sin, by no means clearing the guilty, visiting the iniquity of the fathers upon the children and the children's children to the third and the fourth generation." (Exodus 34:6-7)

Moses wanted to see God's glory, and God agreed to show him. He told Moses to hide in a protective rock, and hidden in the cleft of the rock, Moses saw "behind" the LORD. This was as much of God's glory as he could possibly take in.

God revealed Himself to Moses, and what God tells us about Himself is far more important – and accurate – than what we might think about Him. God introduced Himself to Moses all over again when He said, **The LORD, the LORD God**. This was the same old name for God that Abraham, Isaac, and Jacob knew; this was no new revelation of God. This was the eternal, immutable God. This was more than the stating of a name; it was the revelation of character. God let Moses know who He was – what kind of Person He is, what His nature is – and this was expressed by the name.

First, God is a **merciful and gracious** Person. **Merciful** is better translated "full of compassion." In five of the thirteen times it is used, it is translated "full of compassion" in the New King James Version. The word for **gracious** comes from the idea "to bend or stoop in kindness to an inferior; to favor, or to bestow." It is grace, given to someone who doesn't deserve it.

Second, God is **longsuffering, and abounding in goodness and truth**. **Longsuffering** means that God is slow to anger. He doesn't have a short fuse – contrary to how many people feel God is towards them and others. We all know what it is like to deal with people who have a short fuse - the slightest offense, the slightest perceived wrong, and they are up in arms about it. God isn't like that. He is **longsuffering**.

Third, God is **keeping mercy for thousands, forgiving iniquity and transgression and sin**. God's goodness is shown concretely towards us in His forgiving character. God's goodness isn't just an interesting fact about Him; His goodness makes mercy and forgiveness available to us.

Finally, God is a righteous Person: **by no means clearing the guilty**. If His love and forgiveness are rejected God will punish, and that punishment will have repercussions through the generations that hate Him (Exodus 20:5). His loving, gracious, and giving character does not "cancel out" His righteousness. On this side of the cross we see that because of the work of Jesus, His righteousness is satisfied and grace and mercy are righteously given.

This revelation of the character of God to Moses forever puts away the idea there is a "bad" God of the Old Testament, and a "good" God of the New Testament. God's character of love and mercy and grace is just as present in the Old as in the New Testament. Psalm 86:15 repeats this exact same revelation of God: *But You, O LORD, are a God full of compassion, and gracious, longsuffering and abundant in mercy and truth.* When God revealed Himself to Moses, He did it by proclaiming the truth about Himself. It was certainly a powerful experience, but at its root it was a declaration of truth about God that Moses had to believe and receive. Will you believe it and receive it also?

FORTY-EIGHT
Reading from Exodus: Chapters 34-35

GO FOR THE GLORY

And when Moses had finished speaking with them, he put a veil on his face. But whenever Moses went in before the LORD to speak with Him, he would take the veil off until he came out; and he would come out and speak to the children of Israel whatever he had been commanded. And whenever the children of Israel saw the face of Moses, that the skin of Moses' face shone, then Moses would put the veil on his face again, until he went in to speak with Him. (Exodus 34:33-35)

When Moses came down from Mount Sinai, fresh from his amazing encounter with God, the impact on his life was more than spiritual. There was a physical impact on him also; his face shone with an intense radiance. Exodus 34 tells us that Moses didn't even know his face shone this way, but the people of Israel knew it. In fact, Exodus 34 tells us that when they saw Moses and his shining face, fresh from the radiance of God, they were afraid and they didn't want to come near him. In the last part of our passage, the Hebrew verb for **shone** literally means, "shot forth beams." The word is also related to a Hebrew noun for a "horn." Because of this common relation, the Latin Vulgate mistranslated this verb as "having horns," and so in most medieval works of art, Moses wears a small pair of horns on his head. But the text speaks about glory and veils, and not horns.

Moses, shining face and all, reported to the people all that the LORD told him up on Mount Sinai. Once he finished his words and recorded them – then Moses did something curious. He put a veil over that shining face.

We could easily jump to the assumption that Moses wore the veil so the people wouldn't be afraid to come near him; that it was to protect them from seeing the shining face of Moses. But in the book of 2 Corinthians, God explains to us the real purpose of the veil. It wasn't to hide the shining face of Moses, but it was so that the diminishing glory of his face wouldn't be evident. Moses wore the veil because his shining face *was fading*.

This is how Paul puts it in 2 Corinthians 3:13: *Moses, who put a veil over his face, so that the children of Israel could not look steadily at the end of what was passing away.* The Old Covenant had a glory, but it was a fading glory. God didn't want people to see the *fading* glory of the Old Covenant and lose confidence in Moses. So under God's leading, Moses put the veil over his face. We see this is totally consistent with Exodus 34. Moses came down with the shining face and didn't put the veil on until he spoke to the people, reporting all that the Lord told him on Mount Sinai. Then he put the veil on, to hide the fact that the glory was fading.

The Old Covenant was great and glorious – but it looks pretty pale in comparison to the New Covenant. A bright autumn moon may look beautiful and give great light, but it is nothing compared to the noonday sun. Which light do you live under? When we try to make *our own way* before God, we trust in the same principle at work in the Old Covenant. When we trust *in what Jesus is for us*, and what He did for us, then we live under the New Covenant.

Don't settle for a fading glory.

FORTY-NINE
Reading from Exodus: Chapters 36-37

THE RIGHT WAY TO RECEIVE AN OFFERING

And Moses spoke to all the congregation of the children of Israel, saying, "This is the thing which the LORD commanded, saying: 'Take from among you an offering to the LORD. Whoever is of a willing heart, let him bring it as an offering to the LORD.'" (Exodus 35:4-5)

We've all been annoyed and embarrassed by those who beg for money – whether they be television hucksters or other charities. Few things bring the name of Jesus more shame than ungodly ways of raising money. From the sale of indulgences to the modern television huckster, many have disgraced the cause of Christ through their love of money. Here, Moses showed us the right way to raise money for a godly purpose.

First, there was a command to keep the Sabbath day holy (see Exodus 35:1-3). There will be much for Israel to do in the coming chapters; a complex and exact Tabernacle of meeting must be built. But before they did anything, they had to enter into God's rest by respecting the Sabbath. The same principle holds true for our walk with God today. Anything we do for the LORD must grow out of our rest in Him, and in His finished work on our behalf. Before we give anything to God, we should remember what He gave to us. The Sabbath reminded Israel what God did for them was far more important than what they ever did for Him.

Next, notice how Moses began to receive the offering. He declared, **This is the thing which the LORD commanded**.

The offering was from God's command, not from Moses' clever fund-raising techniques. Receiving offerings is God's "normal" way of channeling funds to His work. God can cause money and materials to just appear by a miracle; yet He almost always chooses to fund His work through the willing gifts of His people. He does this because God's people must learn to be a giving people. One of our great motivations in giving is for *what it does in us* to be givers, not for what it does for others to receive the gift.

Notice who God asked to bring the offerings: **Whoever is of a willing heart**. God wanted gifts from those who <u>wanted</u> to give. God isn't into extortion. For Him, giving is first a matter of the heart, then of the wallet. This idea is echoed in 2 Corinthians 9:7: *So let each one give as he purposes in his heart, not grudgingly or of necessity; for God loves a cheerful giver.*

We also see in Exodus 35:20 how Moses received the offering: *All the congregation of the children of Israel departed from the presence of Moses.* This shows that Moses wasn't into high-pressure giving where people were asked to make a quick, public decision about giving, or to make an immediate pledge. There was no manipulation at all in Moses' request. Moses didn't have a contest pitting one tribe against another, to see which tribe could raise the most money, or any other scheme. God did the work in the hearts of the people. Through the passage, the emphasis is on a willing, joyful giving. Though their hearts were willing, they didn't know what to give, when to give, or how to give until Moses led them. Willing hearts still need to be told when there is a need and how they can meet that need. The willing hearts in Israel gave what they could - not all could give gold or precious gems, but they could give some goat's hair. And certainly, a gift of goat's hair can be just as precious in God's sight as a gift of gold, if it is given with the right heart. What is the condition of your heart? Does your giving show a healthy heart?

FIFTY
Reading from Exodus: Chapters 38-40

GLORY EVERYWHERE

So Moses finished the work. Then the cloud covered the tabernacle of meeting, and the glory of the LORD filled the tabernacle. And Moses was not able to enter the tabernacle of meeting, because the cloud rested above it, and the glory of the LORD filled the tabernacle. (Exodus 40:33-35)

Exodus 40 concludes the building of the tabernacle. When it was finished Moses and his helpers assembled the tent of meeting and God showed His pleasure with their work by blessing it with a display of His glory. Obviously, God was pleased with the obedience of Israel. This was not so much because it showed His superiority over them, but more so because it proved they really did believe Him and love Him. So the glory shone.

Even better than this display of glory was the abiding display of glory. Exodus 40:36-38 tells us that God's glory abided with Israel in the pillar of cloud by day and the pillar of fire by night. He gave them powerful, enduring evidence that He loved them and would not abandon them. It was also proof that God did answer Moses' prayer in Exodus 33:14. There, Moses begged that the LORD would always keep His presence with Israel. So, in answer to that prayer God's presence would be with Israel. This was a promise of His personal presence, not only the presence of His power, provision, and protection - the things He gives. Israel knew God would be with them, even despite the golden calf debacle.

So the Book of Exodus ends with great hope and trust in God. Even though Israel was in the middle of a desolate desert, even though they had fierce enemies waiting for them in the Promised Land and though they were weak and liable to sin and rebellion, God was with them – which was great cause for faith and confidence.

Think about it today. If in the past a "Golden Calf" disaster is behind you, God can still show you His glory and establish His presence with you. If there are many dangers and challenges ahead of you in the next months, God can still show you His glory and establish His presence with you. Let the glory of the Lord accompany you today and in the coming years, as real as a pillar of cloud by day and fire by night.

Great thanks to those who helped with this book. Inga-Lill offered some excellent suggestions and Craig Brewer helped   design the cover, as well as providing the cover photo. Special thanks to those who contributed but didn't want to be named.

David Guzik's Bible commentary is regularly used and trusted by many thousands who want to know the Bible better. Pastors, teachers, class leaders, and everyday Christians find his commentary helpful for their own understanding and explanation of the Bible. David and his wife Inga-Lill live in Santa Barbara, California.

You can email David at
david@enduringword.com

For more resources by David Guzik,
go to www.enduringword.com

City of Lies

The courier

last call

Chaos Walking 703-405-2922

VRS

Rumble
Starchlite
Howmom 29%

CPSIA information can be obtained
at www.ICGtesting.com
Printed in the USA
FSHW010957200320
68261FS